MADE IN FRANCE

MADE IN FRANCE

A Shopper's Guide to France's Best Artisanal Traditions
from Limoges Porcelain to Perfume, Pottery, Textiles, and More

by

Laura Morelli

UNIVERSE

First published in the United States of America in 2008 by Universe Publishing,
A Division of Rizzoli International Publications, Inc.
300 Park Avenue South
New York, NY 10010
www.rizzoliusa.com

Photo credits:
Cover: Baccarat perfume bottle, Limoges cup: © Dawn Smith
Marseille soap: © Laura Morelli
Breton lace, copper pots: © Sarah Nelson
Provençal fabrics, Parisian chandelier: © istockphoto
Title page, acknowledgements, pages 10, 14, 16, 18, 21, 24, 27, 30, 32, 48, 54, 61,
106, 116, 118, 126, 153, 163, 188, 191: © istockphoto
Pages 23, 47: © Salon du Patrimoine Culturel
Pages 34, 40, 62 , 65, 71, 83, 113, 138, 142, 148, 159, 167, 177, 181: © Dawn Smith
Pages 36, 52, 59 (top), 68, 76, 90, 95, 100, 103, 115, 131, 157, 161, 165, 169, 172,
    173, 174, 177, 179, 185: © Laura Morelli
Page 59 (bottom): © Manufacture Nationale de Sèvres
Pages 74, 109, 120: © Mark Morelli
Page 76: © Corbis
Page 79: © Daum
Pages 85, 88, 94, 98: © Sarah Nelson
Page 87, 190: © Martin Schulte-Kellinghaus, CRT Bretagne
Page 110: © Ellen Shea
Page 112: © CRT Centre Henneghien
Page 129: © Patricia Zalamea
Page 133: © Bureau National Interprofessionnel de l'Armagnac
Page 136: © Musée du Beret, Nay
Author photo: Jeff Shaffer

2008 2009 2010 2011 / 10 9 8 7 6 5 4 3 2 1

Distributed in the U.S. trade by
Random House, New York

Printed in China

ISBN-10: 0-7893-1690-0
ISBN-13: 978-0-7893-1690-5

Library of Congress Catalog Control Number: 2007938669

CONTENTS

Merci Bien

The hardest part of writing the "Made In" series is deciding which artisans and retailers end up in print.

For France, this task has been particularly arduous, since the country possesses an astonishing number of world-class craftspeople and artisanal traditions. Literally thousands of potters, weavers, silversmiths, embroiderers, furnituremakers, and other specialists carry on the important job of preserving France's artisanal patrimony, from Limoges porcelain to Baccarat crystal.

In France, many companies, organizations, and individuals helped this project in critical ways. Foremost, I am humbled by the generosity and noble spirit of the people who dedicate their lives to working with their hands and preserving the past, and my sincerest thanks goes to all the craftspeople who shared their time, their vigor, and a little piece of their life's calling with me.

Joseph Bamat, Sarah Nelson, Ellen Shea, and Patricia Zalamea deserve special credit for their diligent research assistance. Thanks go to Lorraine Serra for creating the regional maps. Many thanks to Kaj Grichnik and Myriam Bos for sharing good times and some of the swankiest accommodations in Paris. Thanks also go to Kathleen Jayes, Jacob Lehman, and Joshua Machat at Rizzoli/Universe for making this project a reality. I am grateful to Christy Fletcher for her continuing support.

My family deserves a medal for not only enduring but encouraging my far-flung adventures. *Merci mille fois.*

THE SPIRIT OF TRADITION

I t's excruciating to watch. A young Frenchman in a white shirt and apron picks up a tray of crystal goblets, then tips it into a bin on the factory floor. In one earsplitting second, the glasses shatter into a thousand glistening shards. What makes this destruction especially painful is that these goblets are not just any crystal. They are Baccarat. And with Baccarat, there is no such thing as second-quality. Only perfect pieces reach its showrooms and boutiques across France and around the globe. Anything less than perfect is unceremoniously demolished.

This commitment to excellence exemplifies French artisanship. From faience to flatware, baubles to berets, perfume to porcelain, toys to tapestries, French craftsmanship stands among the most esteemed in the world. I want to take you on a journey through this land whose best artisans, as if by magic, can transform sand into crystal, earth into a gilded teacup, a cocoon into draperies befitting the Sun King, a tree limb into an elegant walking stick, and even frogs' legs—*zut alors!*— into a delicacy.

It's hard for me to admit that it's been so long, but it's true: I have been captivated by France for three decades. I was twelve the first time I laid eyes on the cathedral of Notre Dame in Paris. It sparked a fire somewhere deep inside my soul and ever since, I have returned to France as often as possible to live and work. I studied French in school (I was even mademoiselle présidente of my high-school French Club!). I spent a memorable year at the University of Lyon, and the better part of my graduate school days in Paris archives or traveling to remote sites across the French countryside, from Normandy to the Pyrenees. Years later, I'm still captivated by French art and culture.

During the course of my research for this book, I stood transfixed before artisans who showed me firsthand what's unique about French craftsmanship: beauty, quality, and skill have propelled products like Baccarat crystal, Limoges porcelain, and foie gras to world-class status. In this book, you will meet some of the remarkable people who keep the flame alive for traditions that would have died out centuries ago if it weren't for their singular efforts.

In this paradise of haute cuisine, it is not surprising that many of the country's best handmade items are intended for the table: fine porcelain and china, crystal, cutlery, and exquisite table linens. But lesser-known treasures await discovery in picturesque country villages: the hand-carved walking sticks of the Basque country, rustic pottery and folk furniture in the Alps, and antiques, not to mention artisanally made chocolates and liqueurs.

With this book, I will to lead you to France's best craftspeople, scouring each of its twenty-two regions for time-honored treasures with a uniquely French accent.

VIVE LA TRADITION!

The word *manufacture* conveys a different meaning in French than in English. Originally, in both languages *man-u-facture* connoted "made by hand" or "made manually" (in French, *la main* = hand). In English, the term eventually carried an industrial connotation ("manufacturer" or "factory"), but in French the word *manufacture* retains its original meaning of "made by hand" (the French use another word, *usine*, to mean "industrial factory").

An important feature that distinguishes French craftsmanship is a history of large-scale artisanal enterprises—*manufactures*—employing many skilled craftspeople. The story begins in the eighteenth century with the proliferation of *manufactures royales*, ventures that put the country's best craftspeople to work churning out Gobelins tapestries, Sèvres porcelain, Chantilly lace, and more luxuries—all in the service of the state. Today, many large French corporations with international status—companies like Baccarat, Bernardaud, Daum, even Hermès—still operate in a similar fashion, employing sometimes thousands of highly skilled craftspeople in a *manufacture* where they still make traditional goods, at least in part, by hand.

Of course, in preindustrial society, *everything* was made by hand, even the most banal objects needed for everyday living: wrought-iron tools, pots and spoons, clothing and textiles, and baskets for carrying the harvest. Artisans specializing in an astonishing variety of trades from locksmithing to lace making were indispensable in this society. In France, an insistence on beauty and quality craftsmanship—deeply ingrained in the culture—meant that some of these simple utilitarian works rose to the status of objets d'art.

As avid patrons of the arts, the French monarchy and nobility propelled this demand for beautiful objects, and as a result, craftsmanship flourished to a level nearly unmatched anywhere in Europe. In fact, the French monarchy served as a major patron of handmade goods of the highest order; certain enterprises and

trades, including the Sèvres porcelain *manufacture*, and the tapestry works of Beauvais and Gobelins, owed their very existence to the crown. Of course, French kings,
queens, and nobility were also the main patrons for the silks, trims, and fancy finery that adorned their clothing and their well-appointed residences. Makers of
these luxury goods enjoyed a golden age in the seventeenth and eighteenth centuries, when there seemed to be no limit on royal spending for such items. The
subsequent French Revolution—in part a reaction against royal excess—ousted the
monarchy, emptied the coffers of many French noble families, and put many
craftspeople out of business. Some trades—artisanal wig makers and powderers, for
example—disappeared altogether.

    Artisan families who survived the upheaval of the French Revolution soon
faced an even bigger bouleversement: the industrial revolution. While it improved
life for most, the industrial revolution sounded the death knell for many handmade trades. The nineteenth century ushered in exciting new machines that could
do the work of hundreds of people in just a few minutes. There was no longer a
need for hand-wrought tapestry and lace, since machines could produce rugs and

trims much more quickly and cheaply. Cities and towns that once served as artisanal centers transformed into industrial ones. For example, Lille, in the extreme north, saw its once-renowned handwoven textiles eclipsed by machine-made versions, and while today it remains important to the French economy as a textile center for the fashion and tabletop industries, its craft trade is dead.

When you think about it, it's amazing that certain handmade trades such as metalsmithing, glassblowing, and leatherworking have survived at all. Why have these crafts endured over centuries? What factors have contributed to their success?

One important reason these trades continue is that the French regional and national governments understand the importance of perpetuating their craft patrimony and maintain several initiatives to preserve these important traditions. For nearly a century, artisans have competed for the presitigious triannual Meilleur Ouvrier de France awards from the French ministry of culture, which recognize excellence in various métiers. Recent local and regional projects have also bolstered the craft industry, including a plan to certify and label certain regional crafts (in the same way that fine wines and spirits carry a D.O.C.–type appellation) for the handful of artisans who pass muster. Annual events like the national Journées des Métiers d'Art, in which artisans open their otherwise private ateliers to visitors, help foster awareness and appreciation for these trades. Above all, the tremendous personal and collective pride in carrying on these important trades has been key to their survival.

In addition, thankfully, some French families continue to pass on their knowledge and skills to the younger generation. As far back as the Middle Ages, European craftspeople trained apprentices—either their own children or youths recommended to them—to carry on their trades. To a certain extent this still happens in France, fostered by several national economic initiatives to attract young people to traditional craft trades such as woodworking, metalsmithing, glass and crystal production, and the textile arts.

One of the most powerful forces in the world of crafts today is consumers' voracious appetite for luxury goods. The French are masters of catering to this demographic, and some of the country's oldest, most venerable craft traditions—including leather working and jewelry making—have been propelled to international status in the luxury goods market. Louis Vuitton, Cartier, Hermès, and many others with purely artisanal roots now mostly mass-produce their popular goods (although a few still utilize handmade skills in parts of their processes). In recent decades, multinational conglomerates have snapped up what were once family-run artisan enterprises, creating blockbuster brands but leaving behind the soul, the story, and the people who once crafted these time-honored objects. Fortunately, some of the most recognizable names in French craftsmanship worldwide—Bernardaud porcelain, for example—remain in the hands of the families that founded them, and preserve the original location, the techniques, and most importantly, the *spirit* of their artisanal past.

Meanwhile, tourism—one of France's leading industries—plays a dual role. On one hand, it keeps many artisans in business and fuels enough interest in traditional métiers to keep them alive. The downside, however, is that tourism often cheapens the quality of the wares. Quality-conscious artisans must work extra-hard in the face of stiff competition from those who want to sell lesser-quality goods at a lower price to visitors who may not recognize the difference. One of the goals of this book is to help you distinguish the treasures from the trash, and know what to look for when shopping for a particular object.

Craftmakers, consumers, and the French government thus have all played key parts in the continuation of French artisanal traditions, but it is the singular culture of French artisanship that yields the beautiful objects which, even in our modern world, are a tour de force.

Manufacture: An Artisanal Enterprise

What distinguishes French craftsmanship is a history of large-scale enterprises employing many accomplished artisans in a *manufacture* where goods are—even today—made, at least in part, by hand.

Le Shopping

The French have raised *le shopping* to a high art. Paris and French provincial cities boast some of the most beautiful shopwindow displays in the world, overflowing with chic clothing, mouthwatering delicacies, and alluring objects of every description. Window-shopping is a favorite national pastime for residents and visitors alike.

It pays to understand the peculiarities of French shopping etiquette, which has also been raised to a high art. *La politesse*—politeness—is the crux of French language and culture, and it is extremely important in store etiquette. The American concept that the customer is always right is completely foreign to France; instead, you must *earn* good service. Do your utmost to be as formal and as polite as possible, awkward as it may seem, because it will set the tone for the level of service you receive. It is important to make eye contact with the shop owners as you enter, and greet her or him with a confident, audible *"Bonjour, madame"* or *"Bonjour, monsieur."* A smile goes a long way, even if it is not reciprocated. Over the years, I have gotten a kick out of observing French shoppers who know how to raise *la politesse* to a level of near sarcasm. I could never pretend to be that good, but I've found that as long as you exude deference and graciousness, you will usually get helpful service even if your French is rusty.

Generally, retail stores and small businesses open somewhere between 8:00 and 11:00 A.M. All but the largest stores close for the sacred lunch hour—at least for one hour, but often two—between 12:00 and 3:00 P.M. Then, stores reopen until 7:00 or 8:00 in the evening.

BUSINESS HOURS
French artisans and small shop owners hold notoriously erratic business hours, and on a whim may close for an hour, a day, a week, or even longer. For that reason, I have not posted opening hours in this guide. If there is something you do not want to miss, *always* call ahead to avoid disappointment.

NE TOUCHEZ PAS!
French custom dictates that you should always ask first before touching merchandise in a shop.

What's fabulous about French shopping is that you can enjoy many different kinds of experiences, from historic Parisian department stores like Galeries Lafayette; to haute-couture boutiques like Chanel; to mom-and-pop purveyors of cheese, clocks, lingerie, or chocolate; to producers of Cognac or champagne who welcome you to their private estates; and clamorous street bazaars and treasure-filled flea markets.

In the world of craft shopping, I believe the best possible experience is a visit to an atelier, where you can see for yourself how products are made, and talk directly with the artisan. This interaction is always memorable; you value your souvenir more when you've made a connection with the person who created it. This is not always an option since many artisans work independently in their homes or private studios and distribute their wares to anonymous retail stores. In this book, I have tried to include as many opportunities as possible for you to meet individual crafts-people and observe how objects are made, whether at retail shops, open studios, or annual events. I include retail resellers only if they carry objects that are truly unique or not otherwise accessible.

Factory stores—*magasins d'usine*—offer the opportunity to purchase brand-name items and at the same time to visit the premises to observe how the objects are made. Artisanal wares in France with factory stores include big-name items like Le Jacquard Français, a maker of fine table linens (chapter 2); Daum, the famous crystal house (chapter 2); and Les Olivades and Souleiado, makers of Provençal linens (chapter 6). Some factory stores offer better deals than others. Prices are usually marked down between 10 and 40 percent, but this is off the full retail French prices, so the discount may not be as deep as it seems at first. Keep in mind as well that sometimes factory-store items are flawed or damaged, though this is not necessarily the case.

Many of France's best liqueurs and spirits and other artisanally made culinary products emerge from family-run enterprises, often set on splendid estates that are open to the public. Take advantage of these special opportunities to meet the owners and see how real French people live, to learn about the products and see how they're made, and to purchase items at a discount that is usually significant. Look for signs reading *vente directe* among the regions known for grapes, honey, lavender, or whatever else you are seeking. Tourist offices usually distribute maps showing the main production zones for local food and liqueurs.

Antiquing in France is one of my favorite pastimes, and occasionally you can score a handmade treasure you could not find anywhere else, from ceramic bowls for café au lait to chocolate tins, handwrought wooden balls for playing *boules*, and beautiful crystal and silver. In some of France's top regional antiques centers—

Uzès, L'Isle sur la Sorgue, Tours, Orléans, Angers, and other towns—you might lay your hands on some of the country's top-quality crafts, objects that may be one, two, or even three centuries old. Pay particular attention to antiques dealers who specialize in one area—Limoges porcelain or Basque furniture, for example—as it usually denotes a certain expertise and level of quality. Beyond the shops, check local newsstands for listings of the ubiquitous large antiques shows and events on spring and summer weekends. Also keep an eye out for signs or ads reading *vide grenier* (empty attic). These are essentially garage sales, but that is a totally inaccurate way to describe some of the *trésors* (not to mention *garbage*) that regular people display at these amusing events.

A PRIMER FOR FRENCH SHOPPING

Atelier ouvert: Open studio. An artist or artisan welcomes visitors to see them work.

Fait maison: Homemade. This term usually applies to ice cream, pastries, chocolates, and other delectables.

Magasin d'usine: Factory store.

Production artisanal: Artisanal production. This term means that items are handmade, but it does not always imply good quality.

Vente directe: Direct sale. Usually this applies to producers of champagne, wine, spirits, honey, and other homemade comestibles.

Vide grenier: Empty attic. These community events allow people to get rid of their unwanted items. Though fun, vides greniers are a crapshoot, sometimes amounting to little more than a garage sale, other times yielding incredible treasures.

Marché aux puces: Flea market. One of the most entertaining and unpredictable French shopping experiences.

Excusez-moi de vous déranger—pouvez-vous m'aider, s'il vous plaît?: Excuse me for bothering you—could you please help me? (Believe me, this phrase can open almost any door in France, especially if you are a woman!)

AVOID AUGUST

In some regions, such as Provence and the Côte d'Azur, not much happens between November and April when tourism wanes, and many stores and hotels close during this period. Avoid France at all costs in August, when everybody is on vacation and few stores are open outside of the Riviera, which is mobbed. Again, always call ahead if there's something you don't want to miss.

GETTING IT HOME

Whenever possible, bring your purchases home with you on the plane, preferably in your carry-on luggage. This requires careful planning; I actually pack bubble-wrap when I go to Europe, since it is not easy to find there.

If you've bought more than you can reasonably carry on the plane, opt for an international express mail service like FedEx, UPS, or DHL; you can track the package and have a recourse if something is lost or broken. Don't forget to insure the package, especially if the item is breakable. Some of the shops listed in this book will take care of shipping for you—always ask, since sometimes they have access to special rates.

The French national postal service, *La Poste*, now offers flat-rate packages (labeled *Colissimo*) to overseas destinations. It is not the fastest or most reliable way to ship, but it may be the cheapest. Keep in mind, however, that it will be hard to track your package or file a claim once you're back home. I recently tested this service by mailing two wooden spoons wrapped inside table linens in a large *Colissimo* package to my United States home from a post office in Uzès. It took about two weeks to arrive, and although the linens were no worse for the wear, the spoons were broken. The moral of the story: this service is a good value for non-breakable items.

For larger items like furniture, most French companies use freight brokers to ship overseas. Ask—it may cost less than you think. In my experience, some companies that do a lot of shipping abroad can negotiate special rates with international carriers, which means savings to you.

Once you get home, it's time to face customs officials with your French purchases. The United States, Canada, and Australia all have useful information about customs regulations on their respective federal websites, so be sure to check the guidelines before you leave. In the United States, currently you may bring in up to 800 dollars' worth of purchases for gifts or personal use, per person, duty free. This limit includes two liters of alcoholic beverages; you will pay duty on any additional bottles. You may bring in baked goods, such as croissants, but not fresh cheeses like Camembert or cured meats like jambon de Bayonne; these you'll have to savor while still in France.

How to Use This Guide

Whether you are traveling to France via airplane or armchair, I hope that you will discover something fascinating and valuable in *Made in France*.

This book divides France into six major sections. The first chapter is devoted solely to Paris and its surrounding areas, which could constitute a book in itself. The remaining chapters take France in geographical chunks from north to south: northeast, northwest, the central and eastern regions, southwest, and finally, southeast. Each chapter opens with an overview of the craft traditions unique to each area, then describes those traditions in greater detail.

For ease of locating information, the listings section is divided according to France's twenty-two regions, each of which contains three to eight subregions called *départements*. To include every good craftsperson in each area would turn this project into a multivolume, yellow pages–style directory that would take more than a lifetime to complete; I have focused my efforts instead on listing only the cream of the crop. I have tried to strike a balance between including the major towns and cities where visitors are likely to go and suggesting some off-the-beaten-track locales with fascinating craft traditions you might otherwise miss.

France boasts many excellent small museums devoted to its individual craft traditions, from Nevers faience to *breton* costume, Alsatian pottery, and even berets. Starting with a museum visit is a good way to train your eye, then, when you hit the stores, you'll be able to better recognize good-quality historical reproductions. Some of these museums have shops of their own which often sell modern-day versions of what's in their collections.

For each listing, I provide an address, phone number, and website, if applicable. Obviously, this information is subject to change, so be sure to call ahead. I am not affiliated with any of the enterprises listed in this book, though I have highlighted some of my personal favorites with an asterisk.

LE WEB

Internautes (those who surf the Web) will be happy to know that French artisans and companies have an increasing presence online. Whenever possible, I have included the websites of each enterprise. These sites are in French, though most also have English versions or translations. Sometimes it is possible to purchase goods from the website, but at a minimum, it's a great way to travel virtually to the ateliers of some of France's greatest craftspeople, and it can help you plan your trip.

Finally, a few caveats. There are many excellent guidebooks that lead you to the best hotels, restaurants, and historic sites of France; this is not one of them. I have not included wine or champagne, since it would turn this book into thousands of pages, though a few artisanally made spirits are included in *Made in France*. Rather, I hope to create opportunities for you to meet individual craftspeople and observe how some of France's traditional treasures are made. If you find something you love, and it's not listed in this guide, by all means buy it. Shopping in France is all about discovering beautiful objects that bring *you* pleasure, meaning, and memories of browsing this land of beauty and art.

The goal of *Made in France* is to enhance your appreciation of France's best artisanal traditions, and help you come home with a souvenir you'll treasure for a lifetime. I would love to hear about your experience using this guide, and about the treasures and people you discover in France. Drop me a line at laura@lauramorelli.com. In the meantime, *bonne continuation*!

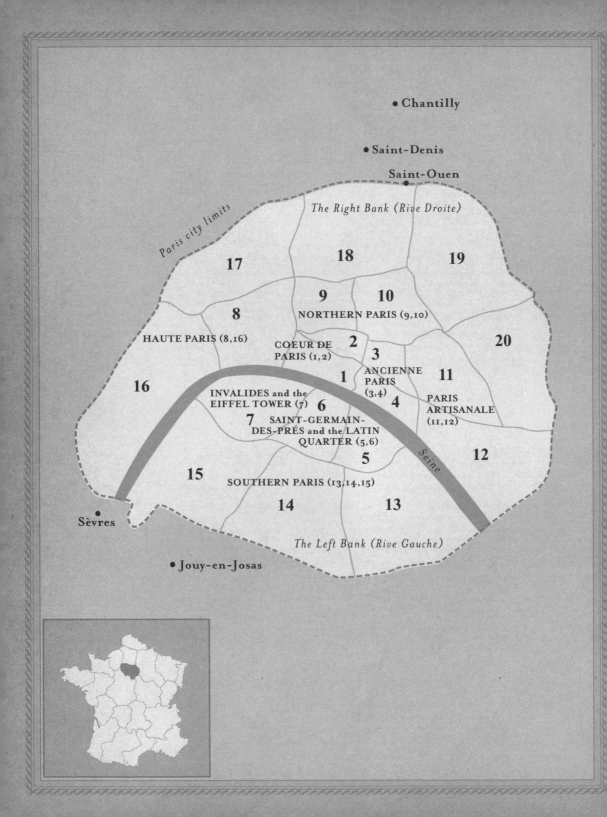

• Chantilly

• Saint-Denis

Saint-Ouen

The Right Bank (Rive Droite)

Paris city limits

17

18

19

9

10

8

NORTHERN PARIS (9,10)

HAUTE PARIS (8,16)

COEUR DE
PARIS (1,2)

2

3

1

ANCIENNE
PARIS
(3,4)

11

16

4

PARIS
ARTISANALE
(11,12)

INVALIDES and the
EIFFEL TOWER (7)

6

20

7

SAINT-GERMAIN-
DES-PRÉS and the LATIN
QUARTER (5,6)

5

Seine

12

15

SOUTHERN PARIS (13,14,15)

• Sèvres

14

13

The Left Bank (Rive Gauche)

• Jouy-en-Josas

Chapter 1

PARIS

P arisian craftspeople are the great *embellisseurs* of the world. Who else but a Parisian could decorate a building, a piece of furniture, or even a woman with such flair and style?

In fact, such embellishment is what distinguishes Paris's craft tradition from others in France. As a capital of haute couture, interior design, and furnishings, the City of Light's best craftspeople work in trades related to those industries—fan and hat makers, perfumers, carvers of gilded frames, casters of drawer pulls, or seamstresses of upholstery trims and custom fabrics. So whether you're seeking a bow for your bonnet, a smart walking stick, a fancy mirror for your boudoir, a tassel for your armoire, or virtually anything else that calls for ornamentation or a stylish finish, let Paris be your oyster.

Traditionally, many of these elaborate embellishments were destined for the city's elite. Through the centuries, the French monarchy and nobility exerted a powerful force on Parisian artisanship. The kings and queens who called Paris home kept thousands of the city's craftspeople busy churning out sparkling jewelry, shimmering interior fabrics and table services, elegant furniture and prestigious coaches, lace collars, custom shoes, and fancy wigs. The monarchy established and patronized France's most famous *manufactures* of porcelain, crystal, and tapestry, some of which still operate under the control of the French government's ministry of culture in and around Paris today. No state building in Paris is without its share of Sèvres porcelain, Gobelins tapestries, and ornately gilded and furnished interiors produced by some of the city's most skilled craftspeople.

In spite of this noble pedigree, thankfully most Parisian specialties have remained within the reach of mere commoners. Paris has been a shopper's paradise since ancient times. By the Middle Ages, trade guilds had already established several important markets, each specializing in a specific métier such as gold, hats, shoes, or baskets. Craftspeople set up shop in certain areas of the city, such as the Left Bank and around the Bastille, and those neighborhoods still flourish today as artisan quarters.

According to popular wisdom, Paris is Paris, and the rest of France is something completely different. To some extent this is true—Paris constitutes its own universe, and claims its own specialties. Fortunately, though, Paris is also the showroom of the provinces. After years of exploring France I am still captivated by the countryside and think it's worth the trek to discover provincial crafts in their native setting, but if you're time-constrained, you can sample the best of the regions in Paris's sleek showrooms and boutiques.

Paris remains a city of neighborhoods, each with a different character. The secret to discovering its most traditional handmade goods is to explore each neighborhood as if it were a small town. The Bastille area, for example, remains a vibrant community of prolific furniture makers, gilders, and frame makers. On the Left Bank, antiques dealers specializing in tapestry, porcelain, and the arts of the table cluster near the Seine. In the nineteenth century, light and airy covered *passages* (covered shopping galleries) appeared on the Right Bank, making for a distinctly Parisian shopping experience; many artisans still set up shop here.

In addition to browsing the city's shops and artisan studios, you can practically make a career of plundering the weekend flea and antiques markets along the outskirts of Paris. Often the most interesting artisanal wares are antiques. These ever-changing extravaganzas of treasure and trash might yield an ornate Rococo mirror, vintage costume jewelry, crystal parts for your chandelier, handmade copper pots, ceramic washbasins, and more.

Over the years I have purchased some of my most beloved objects at the *marchés aux puces* (flea markets): antique silver serving pieces, a door knocker shaped like an elegant lady's hand, and old pieces of Longwy enamel. It's increasingly hard to find bargains, but it's still such a fun experience. The Saint-Ouen market (page 59) is most popular with visitors, but my favorite is the Porte de Vanves (page 57). If you're serious about antiques, check *Revue Alladin*, a monthly magazine that lists all the shows, markets, and auctions in town.

In the listings, I have treated each Parisian neighborhood as if it were a separate village, full of discoveries that await intrepid adventurers who want to discover delightful surprises in the world's undisputed capital of embellishment.

THE TRADITIONS

BRONZE-, SILVER-, AND GOLDSMITHING

Dinanderie, argenterie, et orfèvrerie

T hough not exclusively Parisian, the working of bronze, silver, and gold counts among the city's most highly refined arts. Parisian metalsmiths, perhaps more than any others in the world, know how to raise simple, everyday objects like a picture frame, spoon, or teapot to a work of high art. Bronze sculptures and accents beautify the exteriors of many well-dressed Parisian façades and monuments; some of the best known adorn bridges across the Seine. As you might expect, Parisian bronze- and silversmithing are closely related

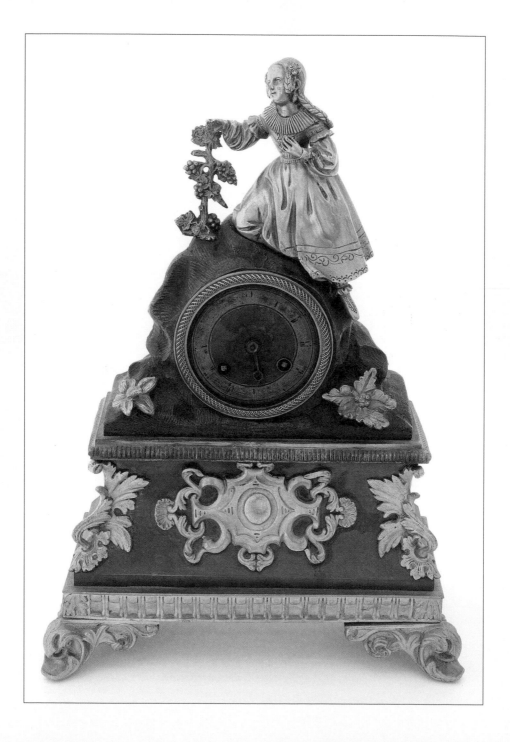

to the world of interiors as well, of which Parisian craftspeople are the undisputed masters. Paired bronze sculptures, often of mythological figures, decorate well-appointed mantelpieces across the city. Ornate bronze chandeliers dripping with crystal teardrops hang from elaborately chiseled ceilings. Period antique tables and chests are adorned with intricately worked bronze accents around the feet, handles, and locks. Tables sparkle with elegant silver place settings and spiral candelabras. This is where the works of French craftspeople literally shine!

Smiths have worked silver and bronze in France since ancient times. The height of Parisian metalworking was the eighteenth century, when these metals became central to stylish interior decoration. Under Louis XIV, furniture embellished with bronze figures, lion faces, masks, chimeras, and swirls became all the rage. The intrinsic value of these natural materials paired with the skill involved in working them make these masterpieces among the most valuable of French craftsmanship.

Silver, bronze, and gold may be cast using the lost-wax process, a technique that has remained basically unchanged since antiquity. The process requires extensive experience with several mediums including wax, pottery, metal, and sometimes wood. The artisan begins by crafting a wax model that is an exact representation of the final piece, often including intricate details. A layer of clay is then spread over the model. When fired, the wax melts, leaving a ceramic mold that becomes a vessel for the molten metal. After it cools, the artisan breaks the mold, revealing the final piece beneath. This basic technique can be refined in infinite ways. For example, to create a hollow bronze object requires creating two nested ceramic pieces, with a small channel between for the wax. Complex or ornate objects, like chandeliers, may be composed of many pieces that are fused together later.

There are other centuries-old trades associated with metal. Gilding involves laying gold leaf over carved wood, or even bronze, to give the impression of solid gold. In France, gilding bronze is considered a specialized and highly prized skill.

Silver- and goldsmithing involve using a variety of hammers to shape a block of metal, called an ingot, into a vessel or jewelry. Beyond the basic skill of raising—hammering a flat sheet of metal over an iron bar to create a hollow form—is a laundry list of specific techniques to add handles or decoration. It's the finishing that is extremely time-consuming and sets Parisian smiths apart for their talent as *ornemantistes*, or masters of ornament.

Today, Paris is home to many excellent individual bronze- and silversmiths, churning out ornate chandeliers and decorative sculptures, as well as professional gilders (those who work in gold) who craft frames and other interior accents.

The city is also home to the world's most esteemed names in silver tableware, including Puiforcat, Christofle, and Odiot Tetard. These historical enterprises still rely on age-old silversmithing techniques and maintain a commitment to quality that truly sets them apart.

L'ORIGINAL

Most French metalsmiths are accustomed to working on commission and can easily create something original for your home.

ÇA COUTE COMBIEN?

Custom bronze, gold, and silver objects can run in the thousands of euros, given the time and skill required to craft them. The good news: Paris antiques markets sometimes turn up less expensive items, like chandeliers and decorative bronzes, that are astonishing for their beauty and uniqueness.

CRÈME DE LA CRÈME

Puiforcat (page 46) and Christofle (page 46), France's most famous silver companies, call Paris home, but the city also boasts several excellent individual silversmiths like Nicolas Marischaël (page 43).

PASSEMENTERIE, TABLE LINENS, AND EMBROIDERY

Passementerie, linge de table, et broderie

I once saw an elegant *parisienne* with a decorative tassel attached to her cell phone, an idea I found *génial* as well as *pratique* for those of us who struggle to dig out our cell phones from the depths of bottomless purses. The art of passementerie, or decorative trim, is a typically Parisian craft. Leave it to the French to invent countless uses for a tassel, whether it's to embellish a pillow, a drapery tieback, a key, or even a cell phone. This knack for detail extends to silk and satin cords, multicolored fringe, twists and braids of velvet and organdy, fabric-colored buttons, and other luxurious minutiae I never knew existed until I visited Paris.

This penchant for passementerie developed alongside the related interior design trades of upholstery and fabric-covered wall decor over the last five centuries. These métiers reached a height of fancy in the eighteenth century, when every square inch of a Parisian noble's residence might be covered with silk fabrics, ornate wall and ceiling moldings, bronze sconces, and crystal chandeliers, not to mention extravagant furniture ornamented with tassels and trims. Today, several French companies perpetuate this specialty of upholstery ornamentation.

Luxurious house linens—including tapestries, bed and table linens, and drapery fabrics—are also a forte of Parisian craftspeople. In the Middle Ages, the drapers' guild counted among the city's most economically and politically powerful trade groups. Today, some of France's most esteemed makers of house linens are still based in Paris. The city became known for tapestry production in the seventeenth century, when the Gobelins tapestry house began supplying the French court with luxurious wall hangings.

Of these home fabrics, one of the most historic and enduring—not to mention most typically Parisian—is *toile de Jouy* (pronounced *twahl de joowee*). You've likely seen countless variations of *toile* in black, red, or beige, printed on a neutral background, depicting scenes of happy peasants. Its heyday was the seventeenth and eighteenth centuries, when the French Compagnie des Indes began importing fabrics from Asia, and Eastern silks with brightly colored landscapes and scenes of daily life became popular in France. French fabric makers were inspired to imitate the style.

In 1759, Parisian fabric printer Christophe-Philippe Oberkampf founded an enterprise in Jouy-en-Josas (hence the name *toile de Jouy*—fabric from Jouy), on the southern outskirts of Paris, near Versailles. Oberkampf's company was tapped as a royal *manufacture* in 1783, which meant that it earned the distinction of supplying the French court with the fruits of its labor. Oberkampf employed Jean-Baptiste Huet, as well as other celebrated artists of the day, to design patterns depicting frolicking peasants, animals, and idyllic country settings, all inspired by Chinese models. Large wooden planks were carved with the pattern and used to print the fabric; one plank was used for each color. Though Oberkampf's factory closed in 1843, the original designs live on as French classics, and today *toile de Jouy* enjoys an enduring vogue in international design.

In addition to these fabrics and accessories made for interiors, other artisanal fabric trades, including embroidery and fanmaking, arose in conjunction with haute couture. Across Paris, several specially trained artisans do nothing but turn out minute masterpieces of embroidery—butterflies, flowers, swirls, birds, and other decorative patterns. These highly prized—and highly priced—little treasures go into service *chez* Chanel, Dior, Christian Lacroix, and other haute-couture designers, where they glitter and flash along the city's runways during its frenzied annual fashion weeks.

L ' O R I G I N A L

Parisian passementerie is one of my favorite souvenirs. Though costly, it's easily portable, so unique, and a simple trick for bringing French style into your home.

Ç A C O U T E C O M B I E N ?

A tassel from one of Paris's top *passementiers* will cost more than you might think. Three yards of tassel trim from Houlès (page 50) set me back more than 100 euros.

C R È M E D E L A C R È M E

If you're a fan of *toile de Jouy*, you'll enjoy the Musée de la Toile de Jouy, in Jouy-en-Josas (page 58). When you're ready to buy, head to Charles Burger (page 39), who preserves many of the old designs from the original Oberkampf factory and reproduces them in contemporary fabrics.

FURNITURE AND WOOD CRAFTS

Menuiserie et ébénisterie

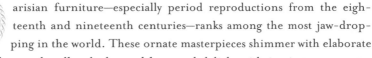

Parisian furniture—especially period reproductions from the eighteenth and nineteenth centuries—ranks among the most jaw-dropping in the world. These ornate masterpieces shimmer with elaborate bronze handles, locks, and legs, and delight with intricate marquetry designs, marvels of craftsmanship.

In the Middle Ages, furniture makers began to cluster along the rue de Cléry and in the Faubourg Saint-Antoine quarter around the Bastille, where the Seine River wends its way south, which made for easy transport of goods. The furniture makers' guild, the Corporation des Menuisiers, required one of the longest and most stringent apprenticeships of all the city's trades and counted several subspecialties. During the golden age of the eighteenth century, a single piece of furniture was often a collaboration of several specialized artisans, including carpenters (*menuisiers*), wood and stone sculptors, metalsmiths, as well as those experienced in particular types of inlay and marquetry (*ébénistes*).

The basic woodworking techniques employed to create furniture, such as crafting dovetail joints, as well as methods to ornament it, such as turning, veneer, and

gilding, have been known since ancient times. Many of the hand tools used in the art of *ébénisterie* also remain the same as in centuries past, including the adze, saw, chisel, and mitre. What distinguishes Parisian furniture is—you guessed it—style and an irresistible urge for ornamentation.

Many of the period reproduction styles most valued today are known for their association with the French monarchy. Among the most coveted are pieces in the feminine style of Louis XV, including chairs with cabriole legs, and commodes, or chests with marquetry and often marble tops. The more classical, reserved styles associated with Directoire and Napoleon are less known abroad, but are highly collectible in France.

L'ORIGINAL

Not even Louis XIV slept in a king-size bed. French antique beds are beautiful, but if you plan to buy one, measure carefully, as they typically run smaller than American frames. However, some French beds will accommodate an American double-size mattress.

ÇA COUTE COMBIEN?

Most French apartments have no closets, so armoires fill an important everyday need. As such, they are not considered luxuries, meaning you can find exceptional deals on these often stunning pieces. Even with shipping, an authentic French armoire will likely cost less than what you would pay for a similar piece back home, and the quality is second to none.

CRÈME DE LA CRÈME

Rinck (page 50), with workshops near the Bastille, handcrafts some of France's most elegant period reproduction furniture.

FASHION ACCESSORIES: GLOVES, UMBRELLAS, JEWELRY, AND MORE

Accessoire de mode

 Parisians possess an unparalleled skill for topping off an outfit with flair, leaving the rest of us feeling fashion-challenged. Paris is the natural habitat of the flaneur, a brilliant term of French origin that describes someone who likes to be seen and show off in public. Is it any wonder then that this capital of couture has nutured thousands of makers of quality accessories, including hats, canes, and umbrellas, through the centuries? After all, to hit the streets of Paris, you must be fashionably prepared.

If you've spent any time in Paris between September and May, you know never to leave home without an umbrella, and you won't be surprised to learn that it was a Parisian who first commercialized the folding *parapluie* around 1710. In the 1760s, the crown granted a company called Maison Antoine—still in business today (page 41)—the right to rent large folding umbrellas. Each was made of taffeta, with a lantern hanging from the inside so that you could recognize the person holding it. By the 1840s, there were some four hundred umbrella makers in the damp French capital.

Prior to the twentieth century, no woman would be seen on the streets of Paris without gloves—perfumed gloves, that is. Glovers in central and southern France began the custom of infusing leather gloves with scent during the Middle Ages; later many of the country's famous *parfumiers et gantiers* (perfumers and glovers)—originally inseparable trades—opened boutiques in the capital. In the eighteenth century, Marie-Antoinette made perfumed gloves all the rage, patronizing several artisans in the city who rocketed to fame on her coattails. Over the course of the nineteenth century perfumers came into their own, and the trades separated, although a couple of Parisian entrepreneurs recently have sought to revive the old concept of perfumer and glover. Today, the majority of French perfume you find in perfumeries and duty-free shops in Paris is mass-produced for the couture houses and luxury-brand conglomerates. Thankfully, however, a few perfumers still concoct signature scents by hand, and one even seeks to revive the tradition of perfumed gloves (page 56).

It's only natural that jewelry making became one of the largest trades of Parisian craftspeople. Jewelers need nothing larger than a hole in the wall, and Paris provides an instant population of consumers, so it's not surprising that so many jewelry makers made their fortunes in fashion-conscious Paris. In the early nineteenth century, the Place Vendôme became the center for the city's most beloved *bijoutiers*. This beautiful square remains the city's most prestigious address for couture jewelers, though most now form part of international luxury brands including Piaget, Chopard, Van Cleef & Arpels, Boucheron, and Chanel; independent artisan jewelers now cluster on the Left Bank.

In addition to umbrellas, gloves, and jewelry, across Paris a few artisans turn out other fashionable accessories—shoes, canes, fans, hats, flower pins, and other wonderful treasures—all by hand. Even in our world of mechanization and mass production, this handful of Parisians operates much the same as in centuries past. You can still find a milliner who will create a hat or bridal veil just for you, a cobbler who will measure your foot and custom make a pair of shoes from scratch, or an artisan who will produce a fancy walking cane adorned with your choice of ebony, ivory, bronze, or silver. *Fantastique!*

L'ORIGINAL
Shoe fanatics come to Paris from as far away as Japan and the United States to have their feet measured by the city's old-fashioned cobblers, who take several months to carefully craft a one-of-a-kind pair of shoes.

ÇA COUTE COMBIEN?
An incredibly realistic handmade flower for your suit or hat will set you back 20 to 100 euros at one of the city's *fleuristes*.

CRÈME DE LA CRÈME
Anne Hoguet (page 52) is the last of the city's fan makers, and Marie Mercié (page 54) has taken handmade hats to new heights of fancy.

SÈVRES PORCELAIN

S èvres porcelain is one of the most typically Parisian souvenirs you can buy. Because of its historical ties with the monarchy and the factory's location on the southwestern outskirts of Paris near Versailles, these refined, beautiful objects have become synonymous with Parisian history and style.

The original porcelain works was founded in 1740 in Vincennes, outside Paris. Louis XV designated it a royal porcelain *manufacture*, and it was later relocated to Sèvres, near the royal palace at Versailles. The *manufacture*'s original strategy was to compete with popular English porcelain and German Meissen ware. Sèvres cranked out bowls, candlesticks, and other wares, mostly for the French court. During its golden age in the eighteenth century, Sèvres had a monopoly on gilded porcelain in France, and its finest pieces were reserved for the court. After the French Revolution, Sèvres became the property of the state, and it remains a national treasure.

Porcelain begins with kaolin, a white mineral that was discovered in France and used to replicate the translucent white finish of Asian pieces imported to Europe in the seventeenth and eighteenth centuries. Sèvres pieces are made of hard- or soft-paste porcelain (*pâte dure* or *pâte tendre*), depending on the percentage of kaolin used. Sometimes pieces are hand-built or thrown on a potter's wheel, but most are formed with plaster molds; the *manufacture*'s collection houses an astonishing ninety thousand molds. The basic pieces are fired to the biscuit stage, when they are then garnished with any surface relief and put in an enamel bath to impart a shiny finish. Refired in the kiln at high temperatures, the pieces are finally ready to be painted and/or gilded by hand.

Sèvres is famous for its several distinct historical colors, including royal blue, turquoise (*bleu celeste*), and even pink (*rose Pompadour*). Classic urns, vases, dishes, plates, and other wares usually had round or oval panels bearing ornate, feminine decoration with figures, flowers, or idyllic pastoral scenes. These pieces were finished off with bright gold gilding on the handles, rims, and bases.

L ' O R I G I N A L
If you know your Sèvres, there are incredible finds among the city's antiques dealers. Be sure to buy from a dealer who specializes in ceramic wares.

Ç A   C O U T E   C O M B I E N ?
For a characteristic Sèvres vase that will transport you back to the anción regime, you will rarely pay less than several hundred euros and sometimes much more, but you can pick up smaller items like cups and saucers for less.

C R È M E   D E   L A   C R È M E
The museumlike Sèvres boutique in Paris (page 40) is a must if you want to see the best Sèvres pieces being made today.

THE LISTINGS

The Seine River cleaves Paris into two halves, the Right Bank (*Rive Droite*) to the north, the Left Bank (*Rive Gauche*) to the south, with the tiny islands of Ile de la Cité and Ile Saint-Louis bobbing in between. Paris has always been a city of neighborhoods, and it retains the flavor of its once-distinct *faubourgs*. Today, the city encompasses twenty administrative districts, or arrondissements, which are indicated by the numbers after each street address below.

THE RIGHT BANK

The *Rive Droite* is home to gentrified, broad avenues; expensive, upscale boutiques and big fashion houses like Chanel, Dior, Givenchy, and Lacroix; as well as the city's top hotels, most esteemed restaurants, and most fabulous department stores.

COEUR DE PARIS:
The 1st and 2nd arrondissements

The 1st and 2nd arrondissements, truly the "heart of Paris," encompass some of the most ancient parts of the city and key institutions, including the Louvre, the Palais-Royal, and the historic market area of Les Halles. This neighborhood also offers some of the city's poshest shopping, from the haute jewelers of the Place Vendôme to the rue du Faubourg Saint-Honoré, housing a retail space for nearly every major global luxury brand as well as a few artisanal makers of fashion accessories. Fine antiques can be discovered at several small streets in the neighborhood as well as the Louvre des Antiquaires, a mall-like collection of museum-quality pieces.

ANTIQUES

*Louvre des Antiquaires
2 Place du Palais Royal, 1st
01 42 97 27 27
www.louvre-antiquaires.com

This is one of my favorite spots in Paris. Even for the most discerning collector, the Louvre des Antiquaires offers an astonishing array of high-quality French antiques, most entirely handcrafted. On any given day, you may find an enamel bowl from Longwy, a rare Baccarat crystal perfume bottle, a chair from the Napoleonic period, or a gorgeous piece of estate jewelry from the coffers of a *grande dame*.

The Louvre des Antiquaires is laid out like an indoor shopping mall with more than 200 retail spaces; each "hall" carries a name like a street name, and each retail space has a unique "address." While the best strategy is to stroll and see what strikes your fancy, the following dealers specialize in traditional French handmade crafts:

Laurent Oiffer
8 Allée Jacob
01 40 20 90 95

This fascinating space overflows with antique corkscrews and other wine-related objects—a find for the serious oenophile!

Pierre Landrieux
5 Allée Canabas
01 42 61 56 48

Antique bronzes, many breathtakingly ornate, glimmer along the display cases and mantle in this small space, interspersed with a few handpicked antique clocks and ceramics.

Galerie V. B. Antiquités
30 Allée Riesener
01 42 61 10 08

This is a prime place to find vintage Sèvres and other important pieces of French porcelain.

Laurence Jantzen
11 Allée Desmalter
01 42 61 58 05

An alluring collection of antique canes and walking sticks from the seventeenth, eighteenth, and nineteenth centuries graces this little space, made with materials as diverse as wood, porcelain, glass, ivory, brass, gold, and tortoiseshell.

Galerie Théorème
20 Allée Jacob
01 40 15 93 23
41/43 Allée Boulle
01 40 15 98 23

A specialist in European and Asian ceramics from the sixteenth, seventeenth, and eighteenth centuries, owner Vincent l'Herrou has assembled one of the city's best collections in his two locations within Louvre des Antiquaires. I have even spied a few museum-quality pieces of Sèvres.

ARTIFICIAL FLOWERS

Etablissements Legeron
20 rue des Petits Champs, 2nd
01 42 96 94 89
www.legeron.com

A fourth-generation maker of incredibly realistic artificial flowers, Bruno Legeron and some ten assistants craft beautiful *fleurs* in silk, cotton, taffeta, organza, and even lace. When Legeron began in the 1880s, it catered to elegant Parisian ladies who ornamented their hats and clothes with flowers; today, the artisans specialize mostly in interior decoration.

CORSETS AND LINGERIE

*Cadolle
255 rue Saint-Honoré, 1st
01 42 60 94 94
4 rue Cambon, 1st
01 42 60 94 22
www.cadolle.com

What a legacy! Poupie Cadolle descends from Herminie Cadolle, the woman who invented the *brassiere*. At the same 1889 World's Fair that unveiled the Eiffel Tower, Madame Cadolle revealed her own novel invention—a traditional corset split into two parts, for a more natural, feminine silhouette. The rest is history. This fifth-generation company carries on the tradition of handcrafting drop-dead beautiful corsets, bras, and other undergarments by hand. The couture house on the rue Saint-Honoré is accessible by appointment only, and fulfills custom orders, including what must be the world's most coveted bridal undergarments. You can view other deluxe lingerie at their ready-to-wear boutique on the rue Cambon.

CRYSTAL

Baccarat Boutique
17 rue de la Paix, 2nd
01 42 44 18 45
www.baccarat.fr

This branch of the Baccarat empire specializes in the fabulous and affordable crystal jewelry that has become popular in recent years, especially among the younger generations.

Daum
4 rue de la Paix, 2nd
01 42 61 25 25
www.daum.fr

Here you can admire the fancy crystal pieces of Daum, famous for its wares made from *pâte de verre*, or glass paste (chapter 2). People either love or hate Daum's characteristic floral designs that harken back to the Art Deco and Art Nouveau periods. If you love them, you'll be in heaven here in the main Paris showroom, which displays a wide range of sculptural objects, tableware, and jewelry.

FABRICS, LACE, AND PASSEMENTERIE

Charles Burger
39 rue des Petits-Champs, 2nd
01 43 44 70 77

Charles Burger is the sole purveyor of historical *toiles de Jouy*, the classic French fabrics depicting frolicking peasants and pastoral scenes. The company has amassed a collection of nineteenth-century leather rolls that once made the ink impressions on fabrics in the old Oberkampf factory, the enterprise that made this style famous. Burger realizes authentic *toile de Jouy* employing those patterns, and also crafts new designs in a similar style.

Declercq Passementiers
15 rue Etienne-Marcel, 1st
01 44 76 90 70
www.declercqpassementiers.fr

Some of the fanciest trimmings in Paris—and that's saying a lot—are lovingly displayed in this shop and museum, now in its sixth generation of family artisanship. In addition to crafting tassels, trims, fringes, and other adornments on commission for private homes, Declercq has been tapped to create, mostly by hand, embellishments for many state buildings. Its craftspeople also have developed a reputation for expertly restoring antique furniture and interiors for châteaux, such as Fontainebleau. Declercq has worked with museum collections as well, including Boston's Museum of Fine Arts, to restore pieces of eighteenth-century French furniture to their original pomp.

Lanel Broderie
20 rue des Petits Champs, 2nd
01 42 97 52 20
www.regislanel.com

Catering almost exclusively to the haute-couture industry, Lanel specializes in details: intricate embroidery trims that appear on the runways of Paris, New York, and Milan as the world's top designers unveil their seasonal collections. Expect to pay several hundred euros for a teeny swoosh or flower, all created by hand in painstaking detail.

Lelièvre
13 rue du Mail, 2nd
01 43 16 88 00
www.lelievre.eu

Lelievre is a distributor of some of the most luxurious home textiles in France. Ask to see the silks of Tassinari & Chatel, the oldest maker of Lyonnais silks still in business today. Founded in 1680, its specialties are handmade curtains, wall coverings, and upholstery fabrics. The company outfitted Europe's royal abodes throughout the eighteenth and nineteenth centuries. Now owned by the luxury-goods conglomerate Missoni, it still relies on careful research to accurately reproduce historical silks, and can custom-make a fabric for you. Tassinari & Chatel also works with museums to restore eighteenth-century French furniture to its original glory. The fabrics are made in an old factory on the outskirts of Lyon, but are only on view at Lelièvre.

Le Jacquard Français
12 rue du Chevalier de Saint George, 1st
01 42 97 40 49
www.le-jacquard-francais.fr

This high-quality brand of typically French table linens from the Lorraine region (chapter 2) is a great souvenir, easy to pack in your suitcase or mail home. You'll treasure this linen every time you throw a dinner party.

Georges Le Manach
31 rue du Quatre Septembre, 2nd
01 47 42 52 94
www.lemanach.fr

In the fifteenth century, the town of Tours, in the Loire Valley, was second only to Lyon as a silk capital. Today, the Manach factory, the Manufacture des Trois Tours, is one of the last producers of these fancy home-decor fabrics and upholstery. The Tours factory, still in the Le Manach family, is not generally accessible to visitors, so this is the only place in France to see and handle these prestigious fabrics. Some of its most popular fabrics are reproductions of patterns made in the eighteenth century, when Asian motifs were popular among the French court. The boutique features a private, exclusive consultation area for one-on-one service, an indication of the custom nature of this enterprise—and its prices.

KNIVES

*Laguiole Boutique
1 place Sainte-Opportune, 1st
01 40 28 09 42
www.forge-de-laguiole.com

A chic, minimalistic display in Les Halles turns all the focus on the handsome knives of La Forge de Laguiole, the company that has singlehandedly revived the centuries-old artisanal tradition of local knife making in Laguiole (chapter 5). The staff is knowledgeable and can point out the details of handmade knives for cheese, steak, golfing, pipe cutting, cigars, and corks. This is a fabulous place to buy if you can't make it to Laguiole, one of France's great knife-making capitals. Prices range from 30 to more than 1,000 euros; they will engrave initials, names, sayings, or anything else you like on the blade at no additional charge. I priced a set of steak knives designed by the prolific Philippe Starck for 450 euros.

LEATHER GOODS

Heller
257–259 rue du Faubourg Saint-Honoré, 1st
01 47 03 99 49

Wander down the alley to the left of this shop's storefront and sneak a peek into this atelier filled with flaps of multicolored hides and old-fashioned leather-working tools. In the shop, I examined a chic gray ostrich bag that sells for 2,000 euros, in line with the prices on this couture street.

PERFUME AND GLOVES

Frédéric Malle
21 and 38 rue de Mont Thabor, 1st
01 42 96 35 13
www.editionsdeparfums.com

See listing, page 45.

Maître Parfumeur et Gantier
5 rue des Capucines, 1st
01 45 44 61 57
www.maitre-parfumeur-et-gantier.com

See listing, page 56.

P. de Nicolai
28 rue de Richelieu, 1st
01 44 55 02 02
www.pnicolai.com

See listing, page 45.

PORCELAIN

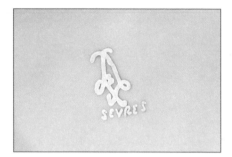

*Manufacture de Sèvres
4 place André Malraux, 1st
01 47 03 40 20
www.manufacturedesevres.culture.gouv.fr

The Paris showroom of the famous royal porcelain maker houses mostly large, one-of-a-kind examples of its signature milky-white production in a museumlike display. Sèvres remains government owned, with most of its current pieces crafted for state affairs and French embassies around the globe.

Manufacture du Palais-Royal
147 galerie de Valois, 1st
01 42 96 21 21

This is one of the city's most renowned makers of porcelain dinnerware. Entire services, from serving dishes to soup bowls and bread plates, constitute sets that are *très traditionnelles*, with many pieces featuring gilded edges, delicate floral patterns, and an elegant sheen. The showy boutique is housed under the gallery of the Palais-Royal, one of the most serene yet prestigious retail addresses in Paris.

Marechal
232 rue de Rivoli, 1st
01 42 60 71 83
www.limogesmarechal.com

If you're going to buy anything along the rue de Rivoli, which is lined with more tourist traps than any other street in Paris, make it a porcelain box from Marechal. Marechal set up shop here in 1934, selling the famous little boxes that its artisans handcraft in Limoges (chapter 4). The main floor specializes in Paris monuments, from the Eiffel Tower to the Arc de Triomphe, but in the back and on the lower level there is a mind-boggling array consisting of thousands of boxes representing everything from jack-o'-lanterns to champagne bottles, shopping bags, picnic baskets, ears of corn, lighthouses, even mummies, which can be had for 100 to 200 euros. Easy to transport, they make great little souvenirs.

SILK

*Prelle
5 place des Victoires, 1st
01 42 36 67 21
www.prelle.com

My favorite urban space in town, the petite place des Victoires is a perfect circle. On its southern side sits the Paris showroom of the prestigious Lyonnais silk maker, Prelle (chapter 4). Prices are commensurate with the quality of these luxurious curtains and table linens, which are crafted using antique looms in the company's historical *manufacture* near Lyon.

STRINGED INSTRUMENTS

R. F. Charle
17 galerie Vero-Dodat, 1st
01 42 33 38 93
www.rfcharle.com

Rosine Charle is the master behind the violins, guitars, banjos, ukeleles, and rarer stringed instruments hanging in this wonderful retail space in the evocative nineteenth-century galerie Vero-Dodat.

TAPESTRIES

Henriette Guichard
8 rue Pyramides, 1st
01 42 60 40 40

Right in the middle of the tourist traps off the rue de Rivoli, Henriette Guichard carries the torch of a family tradition that began in 1907. This third-generation tapestry maker focuses on *fauteuil* seat cushions and footstools. Commission Guichard to make the pillow of your dreams, or a reproduction of one of France's historic tapestries. You can also watch this grande dame at her workbench in the back of the shop.

Tapisserie de France
7 rue Moulins, 1st
01 42 60 65 67
www.tapisseriedefrance.fr

For more than three decades, Annie Bouquet has reproduced antique tapestries, and transformed intricate *petit point* into seat covers for period-style chairs, pillows, and footstools. This closet-size atelier displays some of her best pieces, and you can observe her working on her current project at the rear of the shop. Bouquet works almost exclusively on commission, so if you want to dress up grandma's chair or go home with a one-of-a-kind pillow, this is a great choice.

UMBRELLAS

Maison Antoine
10 avenue de l'Opéra, 1st
01 42 96 01 80

Maison Antoine is one of the last purveyors of the historical Parisian umbrella-making trade. In 1767, Louis XV granted Maison Antoine the authority to rent *parapluies*, and its been in the umbrella business ever since. The cozy shop—in the same location within view of the Opéra since 1885—also carries unique canes, flasks, handbags, and various curiosities. A branch recently opened in Tokyo.

ANCIENNE PARIS:
Saint-Paul and the Marais

The 3rd and 4th arrondissements encompass some of the oldest parts of Paris, including the Ile de la Cité and Ile Saint-Louis, as well as some of its key monuments, such as the cathedral of Notre Dame and the Sainte-Chapelle. Stretching north from the Seine, the neighborhoods of Saint-Paul and the Marais contain some of the city's finest antiques dealers; flags denote the Village Saint-Paul area, with narrow streets and hidden courtyards that house some of the city's nicest antiques shops. Historically, the Marais was a residential area for nobles, but over the last two centuries it has evolved into a multicultural neighborhood with charming restaurants, small museums, and boutique shopping.

ANTIQUES

*Au Passe-Partout
Village Saint-Paul
21 rue Saint-Paul, 4th
01 42 72 94 94

This antiques dealer displays some of the most unique objects I've ever seen in France, and that's saying a lot—I've spent many years exploring the minutiae of French art. In an ever-changing gallery of curiosities, you might uncover a bronze helmet from the Napoleonic era, an eighteenth-century bust, or interesting Roman and medieval ivories, but their specialty is one-of-a-kind wrought-iron hardware and knives from centuries past. Another Au Passe-Partout vitrine at 9 rue Saint-Paul warrants a stroll down this treasure-packed street.

BRONZES AND LIGHT FIXTURES

Delisle
4 rue du Parc-Royal, 3rd
01 42 72 21 34
www.delisle.fr

The Delisle family counts among the city's most esteemed *bronziers*, having supplied decorative bronzes to royal courts around the world for nearly a century and a half. Buy a breathtakingly ornate chandelier or decorative sculpture reproduced from eighteenth-century models off the showroom floor, or commission a one-of-a-kind piece.

FURNITURE

Atelier Michel Germond
78 quai de l'Hôtel de Ville, 4th
01 42 78 04 78

Michel Germond is one of the city's most renowned *ébénistes*, specializing in the painstaking art of marquetry, or veneered and inlay furniture. His forte is Boulle marquetry, a technique developed in Paris during the eighteenth century that employs tortoiseshell and brass in intricate inlay designs. Germond has restored prized pieces for museums and private collectors, and was formerly president of Grands Ateliers, one of France's most esteemed artisan organizations. Despite this impressive pedigree, Germond and his handful of apprentices work in a modest shop along the Seine, filled with sawdust and the tools of their trade.

Meubles Peints
32 rue de Sévigné, 4th
01 42 77 54 60
www.meublespeints.com

If you're a fan of painted furniture, you'll think you died and went to heaven in Muebles Peints, the atelier of Jean-Pierre Besenval, who unearths decrepit armoires and chests from across Alsace, restores them, and then decorates them with folkloric motifs using egg-tempera paint. The shop can arrange shipping outside of France.

QUIMPER FAIENCE

Faïenceries de Quimper HB-Henriot
84 rue Saint Martin, 4th
01 42 71 93 03
www.hb-henriot.com

If you don't have the chance to travel to Brittany, this is a good place to pick up pieces by the region's most esteemed maker of faience, HB-Henriot (chapter 3). Its whimsical, folkloric bowls, plates, and other tableware often feature *bigoudens* and *bigoudines*, the traditionally dressed residents of Brittany.

SAINT-TROPEZ SANDALS

K. Jacques
16 rue Pavée, 4th
01 40 27 03 57

This is one of the few places in Paris where you can find a pair of authentic *tropeziennes*—the characteristic sandals of Saint-Tropez (chapter 6). Although this artisan shoemaker from the Côte d'Azur also sells scarves, boots, and other outerwear more suitable to the Parisian climate, this basic handmade beige leather sandal with straps is its claim to fame. Prices for a pair start at 120 euros.

SILVER

*Argenterie de Turenne
19 rue de Turenne, 4th
01 42 72 04 00

Argenterie de Turenne is a Paris institution. This fun shop brims with vintage silver treasures—old trays, tea services, pots, pitchers, forks, pie servers, and more. Many Parisians come here to replace pieces of their grandparents' services or locate a special wedding gift. Splurge on an entire set once used in a French hotel, or buy just a single fork for 6 euros. You can even pick up silverware by the kilo from the bins on a central table. I scored a set of twelve café spoons here by Christofle for 145 euros.

Cassiopée
Village Saint-Paul
23-25 rue Saint Paul, 4th
01 42 74 00 45

This sparkling shop is tucked inside a courtyard off the rue Saint-Paul. They deal in vintage crystal, silver, and porcelain from France's most renowned makers of the table arts: Daum, Lalique, Christofle, Baccarat, and others. It's a great place to shop for a one-of-a-kind wedding gift.

Nicolas Marischaël
4 rue de Saintonge, 3rd
01 42 78 07 63
www.marischael.com

If you want the chicest teapot on the block, this is the place to find it. Nicolas Marischaël's passion for metalsmithing shines through in his modern, elegant pieces for the table and for home decor. It's also a family affair; Marischaël continues a tradition begun by his grandfather in the 1920s that was passed down through his father.

WALLPAPER

Zuber
5 boulevard des Filles-du-Calvaire, 3rd
01 42 77 95 91
www.zuber.fr

Forget all your preconceived notions about wallpaper before walking into the Paris Zuber showroom. This Alsatian enterprise has been around since the eighteenth century, when scenery on paper began to replace tapestries as wall decoration across France. All hand-printed using antique woodblocks from the Zuber archives, these fabulous trompe l'oeil masterpieces grace the wall of châteaux across France, not to mention the White House, where First Lady Jackie Kennedy installed a series of Zuber scenes in the 1960s. Its Rixheim factory is closed to visitors, so the Paris showroom is the best place to view these exceptional works. Prices are commensurate with the reputation of this house.

HAUTE PARIS:
The 8th and 16th arrondissements

This section of Paris contains some of the city's most exclusive—and expensive—shopping opportunities. All of the top names in *les arts de la table*—Baccarat, Bernardaud, Christofle, Lalique, and others—cluster around the so-called Village Royale between the place de la Concorde and the Madeleine. You can also find some of these items in the *grand magasins*, or department stores, founded in the nineteenth century along the 8th arrondissement's grand boulevards, including Printemps and Galeries Lafayette. The 16th arrondissement is the city's most exclusive residential neighborhood, a haven for fashionable boutiques and artisanal perfumers.

ARTIFICIAL FLOWERS

Trousselier
73 boulevard Haussmann, 8th
01 42 66 16 16
www.trousselier.com

"Silk flowers" hardly begins to describe these incredibly lifelike blossoms, made not only of silk but also crepe, cotton, wood, and other materials. In the atelier behind this boulevard Haussman institution, this family enterprise has been crafting single flowers, such as orchids and roses, as well as stunning arrangements since 1877. Today, they provide bouquets for hotels, banks, weddings, and even government receptions.

CRYSTAL AND GLASS

Baccarat
11 place de la Madeleine, 8th
01 42 65 36 26
11 place des Etats-Unis, 16th
01 40 22 11 00
www.baccarat.com

Baccarat pulls out all the stops in its two-floor Madeleine showroom, presenting a sumptuous, red-velvet display that departs from its more minimalistic stores in Lorraine. The famous crystal maker shows off its most luxurious and costly pieces in these windows, which reflect the columns of La Madeleine. You can spend close to 5,000 euros on a small vase; for more modest budgets, fashionable pendants and rings can be had for 100 to 200 euros. The place des Etats-Unis is Baccarat's Paris headquarters, and its boutique, too, proffers an extravagant setting.

Lalique
11 rue Royale, 8th
01 53 05 12 12
www.cristallalique.fr

This is the flagship store and headquarters of the eponymous glassworks founded by the famous artist René Lalique. Here you can pick up some of the company's signature works in *pâte de verre*, from figural sculpture to tableware and more recently, funky jewelry. Every piece of Lalique is hand-produced in its *manufacture* in Wingen-sur-Moder, in Alsace, but it is not accessible to visitors, so come to the Parisian showroom to bask in the glory of these translucent *objets*. Prices are lower than in the United States, but not cheap any way you slice it. The store ships.

Saint-Louis
13 rue Royale, 8th
01 40 17 01 74

This old crystal-making house based in Lorraine dates to the sixteenth century. Now affiliated with Hermès (chapter 2), Saint-Louis runs an upscale boutique displaying the best of its fancy lead-crystal designs.

Gien Faience
Gien Boutique
18 rue de l'Arcade, 8th
01 42 66 52 32
www.gien.com

See listing, page 53.

KNIVES

Laguiole Boutique
29 rue Boissy d'Anglas, 8th
01 40 06 09 73

See listing, page 40.

LINENS

D. Porthault
50 avenue Montaigne, 8th
01 47 20 75 25

The mother of the current proprietor, Marc Porthault, founded this enterprise, and it has quickly risen to the top of the competitive Parisian house-linen hierarchy. With clients ranging from the White House to Windsor Castle, Porthault exudes luxury and quality from its crisp tablecloths to the monogrammed bed linens. Part of the process is still done by hand, including embroidery and stitching.

Noël

1 avenue Pierre Ier de Serbie, 8th
01 40 70 14 63
www.noel-paris.com

Noël is one of the city's most exclusive addresses for table and house linens. Drawing from an archive of some thirteen thousand embroidery designs—some historical, some the creation of the Noël family over the course of the early twentieth century—its embroiderers use hand techniques, looms, as well as hand-guided machine embroidery to craft elegant and classic table, bed, and baby linens. In the 1980s, the company passed out of the hands of the Noël family, but thankfully the current owners continue this venerable tradition. Bring in your ideas and have them create a custom design for you.

MUSTARD

Maille

6 place de la Madeleine, 8th
01 40 15 06 00
www.maille.com

Bedazzled by the lavish store windows of Baccarat and the delectables of food purveyor Fauchon, you may miss the unassuming shop of Maille, Dijon's famous mustard maker. Stop in for a few little jars of the tasty condiment, and be sure to check out the little ceramic mustard pots created espcially for Maille by artisans in some of France's most renowned ceramics centers, including Moustiers-Sainte-Marie (chapter 6) and HB-Henriot of Quimper (chapter 3). Most come with mustard spoons of wood or porcelain.

PERFUME

Frédéric Malle

140 avenue Victor Hugo, 16th
01 45 05 39 02
www.editionsdeparfums.com

This branch of Frédéric Malle is located on one of the chicest residential streets in Paris. The grandson of the founder of Christian Dior's perfume line, Malle has established a small empire, distributing his perfumes in department stores and boutiques around the world. The enterprise remains artisanal, however, relying on the expertise of nine of France's most distinguished "noses" to develop the signature scents. The understated decor features "horns" along the wall in which you insert your face to fully internalize each fragrance. Ask about commissioning a custom perfume.

P. de Nicolai

69 avenue Raymond Poincaré, 16th
01 47 55 90 44
www.pnicolai.com

In a much more clinical setting than Malle, Patricia de Nicolai, a descendant of the Guerlain perfume family, concocts custom scents in her bright, back-of-the-shop *laboratoire* visible through glass windows. Spray her signature samples on the white strips (*échantillons*) scattered along the counter, and sniff. Prices are reasonable, with many bottles ranging between 20 and 100 euros. If none of these strikes your fancy, you can commission a personal scent to be created just for you.

PORCELAIN

Bernardaud

11 rue Royale, 8th
01 47 42 82 66
www.bernardaud.com

Located alongside Gucci and Maxim's, the Paris boutique of this famous Limoges porcelain maker features some of its loveliest pieces. A special section displays hand-finished reproductions of historical cups, saucers, and teapots from the seventeenth and eighteenth centuries. The back gallery specializes in Bernardaud's line of porcelain jewelry, which is also worn by the sales staff. For around 200 euros, I purchased a set of six espresso cups and saucers in a coral and gold pattern, beautifully encased in the company's signature round turquoise hatbox. This branch of Bernardaud also distributes Ancienne Manufacture Royale de Limoges, another of Limoges's oldest, most distinguished porcelain makers (chapter 4).

Haviland
25 rue Royale, 8th
01 42 66 36 36
www.haviland-limoges.com

Haviland, porcelain from Limoges, is distributed in department stores in France and abroad, and is even available in the duty-free shops at Charles de Gaulle airport—but why not buy it from one of Paris's swankiest boutiques? More colorful and fussy than the understated Bernardaud down the street, Haviland's wares appeal to those of more whimsical taste.

SILVER

*Christofle
9 rue Royale, 8th
01 55 27 99 13
www.christofle.com

This is an absolutely gorgeous store, the most luxurious of Christofle's retail outlets in France. Christofle is known for its fine-quality silver and silverplate; the best hotels in France use its tableware, and a gift from Christofle is always appreciated. A lovely display showcases pieces from Christofle's nearly two-hundred-year history, and downstairs you can admire fully decorated tables pairing Christofle silver with Limoges porcelain and Baccarat crystal. I drooled over the contemporary teapots and more traditional silver trays and pitchers, but my favorite items are the ice buckets embellished with shiny flowers. There are no bargains here, but if possible, take advantage of the *détaxe*—in which tax is removed for residents of countries outside the European Union.

*Odiot Tetard 1690
7 place de la Madeleine, 8th
01 42 65 00 95
www.odiot.com

Truly the crème de la crème of gold and silver implements for your table, Odiot Tetard can outfit you with France's fanciest tableware. Unfortunately, the atelier of these masterful artisans is not open to the public, but you can appreciate the results of their labor in its showroom, one of Paris's most elegant retail spaces. Two floors are devoted to the exquisite gold and silver works, including the showy table displays that Odiot has been making since 1690 for heads of state around the world (as well as mere mortals with fine taste and large budgets).

Puiforcat
48 avenue Gabriel, 8th
01 45 63 10 10
www.puiforcat.com

Since 1993, this venerable silversmithing house has been owned by luxury-goods maker Hermès and distributed in stores around the world. Puiforcat's only eponymous store is a wonderland of gorgeous silver objects. Though founded in the nineteenth century, it wasn't until the 1920s and 1930s that Jean Puiforcat brought the company to fame. A single piece from this era fetches tens of thousands of dollars at auction, and museums around the world avidly collect works handmade in this prestigious silverworks in Saint-Denis, on the outskirts of the city (page 59).

STAINED GLASS

Atelier d'Art Saint-Didier
40 rue Saint-Didier, 16th
01 47 04 78 75
www.atelier-saint-didier.com

For a firsthand look at the fascinating techniques of glass art, peer down into this below-street-level atelier of stained glass. Here Caroline Prégermain, a Meilleur Ouvrier de France award winner, realizes custom projects such as panels and screens for museums and private clients.

PARIS ARTISANALE:
The Bastille, 11th and 12th arrondissements

Far from the luxury showplaces of the 1st and 8th arrondissements, this no-frills section of town features hole-in-the-wall studios where some of the country's best *ébénistes* craft stunning furnishings ranging from chairs to chests. Historically a bustling artisan quarter and a center of furniture making, the old

Faubourg Saint-Antoine and the Bastille, the 11th and 12th arrondissements are still home to hundreds of craftspeople.

If you have limited time, head straight for the Viaduc des Arts, which runs along the rue Avenue Daumesnil near the Gare de Lyon. In the 1990s, the French government renovated this old viaduct, part of the nineteenth-century railroad that linked Paris and Vincennes. Under the archways, some fifty artisan studios opened in a half-mile stretch along avenue Daumesnil, attracting craftspeople from the provinces. You can spend an enriching hour or two browsing these little gems, as this is one of the best places in Paris to see craftspeople at work.

ANTIQUE LINENS

Marie Lavande
83 avenue Daumesnil, 12th
01 44 67 78 78
www.marie-lavande.com

This absolutely fascinating shop contains a series of long tables where fabric conservators carry out the painstaking craft of preserving antique lace and table and house linens. Joëlle Serres lovingly takes in a vintage church vestment, a lace mantle, a tablecloth wrested from a provincial château, and countless other treasures as if they were stray cats in need of care. Whether organdy, cotton, linen, or other material, her conservators nurse each thread back to health. Select pieces are for sale.

ARTIFICIAL FLOWERS

Guillet
1 bis avenue Daumesnil, 12th
01 43 40 80 00

Since 1896, the Guillet atelier has toiled at producing amazingly realistic flowers in cotton, silk, and other materials. In addition to crafting single flowers to adorn hats, lapels, and jewelry, Guillet also creates fantastic floral displays for the Paris theaters and cinema houses.

BOOKBINDING

Jacky Vignon
2 rue Gonnet, 11th
01 44 64 78 28

Jacky Vignon is one of the city's most authentic old-world artisans, quietly upholding the once-prolific trade of *reliure*, or bookbinding. Vignon crafts fine leather bookbindings that find loving homes in France's historic libraries, institutions, and private collections. Using a variety of skins, decorative papers, and gilded details, Vignon patiently fashions a unique binding for each treasure that crosses his desk. The atelier is wedged between a furniture restorer and shoe repair shop in this no-frills artisan district. Vignon also displays some of his work in an exhibition space at 303 rue du Faubourg Saint-Antoine.

BRONZES

BFA Créations
22 rue Trousseau, IIth
01 48 06 79 79
www.bfa-creations.fr

I drooled over the wall sconces with black and
red crystal teardrops in BFA Creations's
bright, elegant showroom. Classy bronze
chandeliers and other handmade fixtures of
bronze are finished with gilding and rich
crystal accents. For a personal statement, you
can order a custom fixture, choosing everything from the basic materials to the lampshades and lightbulbs. The shop is located
across from Les Passementeries de I'Ile de
France (see page 51).

Baguès
73 avenue Daumesnil, I2th
01 43 41 53 53
www.bagues-france.com

Look down, and you'll think you're in a warehouse, with cardboard boxes, bubble wrap, and
packaging strewn all over the bare floor. Look
up, and you'll realize you're in a wonderland
glimmering with bronze chandeliers, lamps,
sconces, and the most incredible pirate ship
chandelier overhead. Baguès has created historical reproductions for Versailles, as well as
many other institutional and private collectors
across France and around the world.

Quincaillerie Au Progrès

11 bis rue Faidherbe, 11th
01 43 71 70 61
www.auprogres.net

Quincaillerie d'art, or artistic hardware, hardly describes the ornate treasures that this establishment produces. Drawer pulls, decorative swirls, and other hardware for the adornment of both period furniture and interiors are their specialty. Whether of bronze, pewter, gold, or iron, the little marvels organized in tiny drawers and displayed upon the wall make a feast for the eyes. Purchase an eagle or caryatid escutcheon for your Louis XVI chair, or a more understated round drawer pull for your grandmother's Empire chest of drawers. This establishment has served the Paris furniture trade since 1873.

Série Rare

121 avenue Daumesnil, 12th
01 55 42 92 10

If you want a doorknob, drawer pull, curtain tieback, or sconce that is truly different, this is the place. A small team of metalsmiths at Série Rare turns out beautifully artful hardware for interior design, including lamps, frames, and one-of-a-kind door handles in pewter and other metals. Looking for a custom towel rack? No problem. They also design special pendants and brooches that are surprisingly affordable, starting at 44 euros. They operate another showroom at 6 rue de l'Odéon in the 6th arrondissement.

DOLLS

Automates et Poupées

97 avenue Daumesnil, 12th
01 43 42 22 33
www.automatesetpoupees.com

There's no denying that antique-doll repair shops are weird, what with all those pairs of eyes staring at you as you browse. But whether you want to fix your grandmother's music box or commission a custom-made doll with blinking eyes or moving arms, this is one of the world's best places to do it. One of their specialties is chirping birds made using a multitude of materials including real bird feathers.

FRAMES AND GOLD LEAF

Atelier Lebeau

117 avenue Daumesnil, 12th
01 43 45 96 05

An outrageously ornate wooden chandelier lured me into this otherwise no-frills workshop along the Viaduc des Arts. These master craftspeople show off their wood-carving skills in the creation and restoration of gorgeous frames that are sculpted and gilded. This family business boasts the Musée d'Orsay and the Musée Carnavalet among an exclusive clientele.

Maison de la Dorure

87 avenue Daumesnil, 12th
01 44 75 96 96
www.maisondeladorure.com

Gold leaf is the specialty of this frame-making shop, whose artisans rely on eighteenth-century models as the inspiration for the classic, ornate frames in their showroom. From a catalogue of more than three hundred models, you can select one that's right for you. They also create gilded decorative ornaments for furniture and interior decoration, as well as jewelry using gold leaf.

FURNITURE

Claude Balcaen

39 avenue Daumesnil, 12th
01 43 44 10 54
www.mobilier-balcaen.com

If you're shopping for a reproduction chaise, this is a great place to buy. First select a basic chair style, then pick a stain, a paint, or even gilding in twenty-two-karat gold. Next, choose a fabric for the upholstery. Balcaen can whip up a *fauteuil, canapé,* or *bergère,* just as it looked in the days of Louis XIV or Napoleon. Expect to pay 4,000 to 7,000 euros for a stunning finished piece.

*Jean-Michel Dissidi
16 passage de la Bonne-Graine, 11th
01 47 00 47 95
www.dissidi.com

Dissidi's furniture epitomizes Parisian style: ornate and elegant with an unparalleled *hauteur*. This warm, welcoming studio specializes in reproduction period furniture from the eighteenth and nineteenth centuries, with gold accents, intricate inlay, and richly embroidered fabrics and embellishments. Ornate wainscoting and other feats of woodworking decorate this showplace of high refinement.

*Rinck
8 passage de la Bonne-Graine, 11th
01 47 00 42 67
www.rinck.fr

If you visit one furniture maker in France, make it Rinck. Its showroom is a little jewel box on a quiet side alley in the Bastille quarter; the few pieces displayed here give a hint of the immense talent that lies behind this atelier, in business since 1841. Rinck's collaborative craftspeople are absolute masters of their respective trades: marquetry, ornamental sculpture, chiseling, woodworking, carpentry, and metalsmithing. Period reproductions are their main focus, but they also make custom cabinetry and wall ornamentation that is some of the finest interior work around. Nearly everything is made to order, for a client list that includes heads of state and rock stars. In 2003, Rinck was acquired by Atelier Thierry Goux, another woodworking enterprise, and we can only hope that the Rinck quality and tradition will persist.

Soubrier
14 rue de Reuilly, 12th
01 43 72 93 71

Soubrier is an old-fashioned Parisian furniture maker and purveyor of gorgeous traditional home decor. The showroom features ornate reproductions of classic eighteenth-century tables and commodes. In the courtyard, look for the atelier entrance, where you can glimpse master furniture makers at work on this painstaking craft. Prices—reflecting the quality—are high.

LAMPSHADES

Atelier de Marie
10 rue de Charonne, 11th
01 49 29 74 44
www.latelierdemarie.com

Custom lampshades, or *abats-jours*, are the focus of this inviting atelier. Whether pleated, embroidered, with or without trim, satin, tulle, or voile, if you don't find a lampshade that strikes your fancy, you can have one made. Bring in your grandmother's lamp and the artisans here will craft a new shade for it. You can also buy lamp bases in alabaster, wood, or ceramic off the shelf, starting at around 75 euros.

LEATHER GOODS

Maison Fey
15 avenue Daumesnil, 12th
01 43 41 22 22
www.maisonfey.com

Maison Fey turns out some of the most colorful leather goods I've ever seen—even decorative sheafs of white and fuschia punched with gilded birds and flowers. More traditional desk accessories like mail files and pencil holders round out the collection; one of its most popular items is a magazine file disguised as a stack of books with gilded bindings, which sells for around 100 euros. Fey also makes small pieces of furniture, such as chests of drawers or side tables, which run around 650 euros.

PASSEMENTERIE

*Houlès
18 rue Saint Nicolas, 12th
01 43 44 65 19
www.houles.com

It's hard to get more chic than this. Houlès is one of the country's most esteemed makers of passementerie, or upholstery and decorative trims. Based in Saint-Etienne, a city near Lyon once renowned for this craft, the Paris showroom is its only outlet accessible to both the public and the trade, each with different opening hours. Houlès has been supporting the furniture trade since 1928, and is now in its fourth generation of family ownership.

Les Passementeries de L'Ile de France

11 rue Trousseau, 11th
01 48 05 44 33
www.pidf.fr

This lovely showroom displays a mere fraction of this well-regarded *passementier*'s work. Robert Oberti and Marie-Claude Doudoux-Oberti run this family enterprise founded in 1926. The factory is situated due north of Paris in Belloy-en-France, a Picard village with a five-century-old tradition of passementerie. Some sixty specialists work by hand and on historical looms to weave tassels for window dressings and throw pillows, pompoms, fringe, curtain cord tiebacks, and other trims from cotton, silk, wool, and other fibers. The company's special commissions include decorating high-end hotels and the historic restoration of the Opera of Monte Carlo.

PORCELAIN

Atelier Le Tallec

93–95 avenue Daumesnil, 12th
01 43 40 61 55
www.atelierletallec.com

I love this shop because you can watch ceramicists at work at their tables under the archway. Atelier Le Tallec began its life in the 20th arrondissement back in 1928, when Camille Le Tallec took over his father's porcelain shop. Today, a dozen or so artisans carry on the painting of traditional French porcelain. They work from designs of various porcelain centers, especially Limoges, replicating designs of the eighteenth and nineteenth centuries. You can order a custom piece or service.

SHOES

Norayr Djoulfayan

3 bis rue Jules Vallès, 11th
01 43 71 97 48

This artisan-*bottier* follows, literally, in his father's footsteps. Norayr Djoulfayan set up a shoe shop in this rough-and-tumble quarter in 1977. From this humble atelier, he has built an international reputation for his custom-made men's and women's leather footwear. Behind his workbench is draped an enormous alligator skin, and other leather samples in a rainbow of colors hang from the walls. Djoulfayan patiently explains the qualities of each type of leather and can advise you on the perfect pair of shoes for your foot. A handful of samples in the window will give you some ideas, or bring your own design. Either way, expect to pay 600 to 1,300 euros per pair with a wait of at least a few weeks. Clients come from as far away as the United States and Japan to ask this master to work his magic.

NORTHERN PARIS:
9th and 10th arrondissements

These areas hold neither glitz nor charm, but are worth a detour for an antiques district and a smattering of old-world trades. The so-called Quartier Drouot boasts several dozen antiques dealers clustered around Drouot auction house, and a group of china and crystal purveyors gather along the rue de Paradis.

CANES

Galerie Segas

34 passage Jouffroy, 9th
01 47 70 89 65
www.canesegas.com

A true cabinet of curiosities and one of the most fascinating displays in Paris, this shop specializing in handmade antique canes and walking sticks will spark your imagination. Gilbert Segas and family collect antique handmade canes incorporating everything from ivory to ceramic, crystal, and hundreds of different woods. Look for the moose antlers hanging above the entry to this red-velvet interior, with a fountainlike spray of canes in the window. The shop is located in the passage Jouffroy, one of the city's most evocative *passages*, or covered shopping galleries.

FANS

Anne Hoguet
2 boulevard de Strasbourg, 10th
01 42 08 19 89
www.annehoguet.fr

The last of a dying breed, Anne Hoguet carries on the once-vibrant tradition of fan making. The fourth generation of her family to work in this craft, Hoguet offers up part of her workshop as a museum, exhibiting antique fans from all over the globe made of materials as diverse as lace, paper, feathers, and plastic. Though she works regularly for some of the city's top couture houses, she can make a model for you in various papers, feathers, or fabrics, at prices that are surprisingly reasonable.

LACE AND EMBROIDERY

Lesage Paris
13 rue Grange Batelière, 9th
01 44 79 00 88
www.lesage-paris.com

Masters of embroidery for haute couture, Lesage is famous for the sparkly embellishments that adorn the creations of Dior, Balenciaga, and other famous fashion designers. Lesage's intricate embroidery patterns put sequins, pearls, and gems to glamorous effect. In 1924, Albert Lesage bought an embroidery company that dated back to the Second Empire, and today the firm relies on a library of an astonishing sixty thousand samples. You can even take a course here, in French or English, to learn how to create haute-couture embroidery.

PERFUME

Musée de la Parfumerie Fragonard
9 rue Scribe, 9th
01 47 42 04 56
www.fragonard.com

Fragonard is a famous perfumer from Grasse, France's perfume capital in Provence (chapter 6). After visiting the museum steps away from the Opéra, you can sample the floral scents of this maker and purchase some at reasonable prices.

SILVER

Olivier Antiquités
63 passage Jouffroy, 9th
01 45 23 26 23

This dealer in antique silver displays choice pieces in a striking window arrangement that uses green velvet to highlight these shining works of craftsmanship. Select pitchers, platters, and salt cellars from important French silvermaking centers, including Paris and Orléans, are dramatically lit so that you can clearly see the engraved hallmarks so essential to valuing silver.

THE LEFT BANK
(Rive Gauche)

The Left Bank conjures images of intellectuals debating philosophy over a sidewalk café table, an Impressionist painter creating masterpieces in a crooked garret, and men playing boules in the Luxembourg Gardens. In recent years, however, international brands have begun to sneak soulless boutiques into this quaint neighborhood. The good news: the Left Bank remains Paris's intellectual and artistic hub, and excellent old-fashioned craft shopping opportunities still abound.

SAINT-GERMAIN-DES-PRÉS AND THE LATIN QUARTER:
5th and 6th arrondissements

Saint-Germain-des-Prés has the feel of a small town within a big city and is one of my favorite parts of Paris. It's hard to imagine how many thousands of university students have pounded the pavement of the Latin Quarter since the University of Paris opened its doors in the thirteenth century. The Sorbonne, or *Paris Quatre*, as the students call it, still breathes life into this pulsating maze of cobblestoned streets and broad avenues. Together, the 5th and 6th arrondissements boast some of Paris's cutest and most historic shops. Important antiques dealers cluster in the Village Suisse along the avenue de la Motte-Piquet, and the Carré Rive Gauche, behind the Musée d'Orsay.

CHOCOLATE TINS

Ladurée
21 rue Bonaparte, 6th
01 44 07 64 87
www.laduree.fr

With several prestigious addresses in Paris, not to mention its own counter in Harrod's department store in London, Ladurée is hardly a secret. I highlight its rue Bonaparte location, though, for its wonderful exhibition of historic handmade tin molds used to create the chocolate that has made this Parisian *confissier* famous. While waiting for a table in the tearoom, you can admire hundreds of forms, from enormous eggs to miniature soldiers, displayed behind glass.

The tins are not for sale, but the delectable pastries are, so enjoy!

FAIENCE

*Gien Boutique
13 rue Jacob, 6th
01 46 33 46 72
www.gien.com/fr

This stone-walled showroom for one of France's best-loved provincial crafts—Gien faience (chapter 4)—is full of ambience. Located in the Centre region, Gien's faience is known for its bright colors, with bold floral patterns in predominant tones of burgundy and blue. A fine selection of tableware patterns, as well as pieces for display only, pair nicely with table linens by Le Jacquard Français (chapter 2). The staff is friendly and speaks English.

LAMPSHADES

L'Ancolie
18 rue de la Sourdiére, 5th
01 40 46 97 11
www.ancolie-paris.com

Working in a modest atelier within view of Notre Dame cathedral, Georgie Guilleman creates lampshades (*abats-jour*) that are the stuff of your dreams. You can have an old lamp redone, or transform any of the hand-picked decorative objects in the store, many animal-themed, into a unique light fixture.

LEAD SOLDIERS

Au Plat d'Etain
16 rue Guisarde, 6th
01 43 54 32 06
www.auplatdetain.com

One of Paris's oldest continuously operating stores, Au Plat d'Etain has been crafting miniature hand-painted lead soldiers since the days of *La Révolution* in 1775. You can pick up a single soldier for around 5 euros, but plan on spending at least 100 for a set. Although they carry figurines from clowns to World War II flying aces, a French Revolution figure makes a classic and easily transportable souvenir from one of the city's most nostalgic shops.

LYONNAIS SILKS

Lelièvre
4 rue de Furstenberg, 6th
01 44 07 53 10
www.lelievre.eu

See listing, page 39.

MILLINERY

*Marie Mercié
23 rue Saint-Sulpice, 6th
01 43 26 45 83

Forget everything you ever knew about hats. The headgear of Marie Mercié will challenge and delight your senses, and you may just come away with one of Paris's most unique wearable handmade objects. Whimsy and drama characterize the selection of this delectable boutique. One hat reminded me of a mushroom, another of a toy boat. I finally settled on a square beret in frosty green, with a button on the top. Prices run from 200 to 900 euros for a hat, more for a *chapeau sur mésure* or other custom work such as bridal veils.

PROVENÇAL LINENS

Les Olivades
95 rue de Seine, 6th
01 43 54 14 54
1 rue Tournon, 6th
01 43 54 14 54
www.lesolivades.com

Compared to the boutiques of this fabric maker in its native Provence (chapter 6), the emphasis in the Paris showrooms is fashion. You can buy collared shirts, ties, skirts, and other prêt-à-porter in Les Olivades' characteristic prints, in the 100 to 200 euro price range.

Souleiado
78 rue de Seine, 6th
01 43 54 62 25
1 rue Lobineau, 6th
01 44 07 33 81
www.souleiado.com

Like the nearby branches of Les Olivades, this Provençal maker of fancy fabrics highlights its ready-to-wear collection in its Paris boutiques. These fabrics feature its signature colors—periwinkle blue, marigold, kelly green, and tan.

SAVON DE MARSEILLE

La Compagnie de Provence
5 rue Bréa, 6th
01 43 26 39 53
www.lcdpmarseille.com

This *Marseillais* company (chapter 6) has jazzed up a rather lackluster trade—soap making—with sleek merchandising and nice packaging that will make a unique French gift. At its headquarters in Marseille, soap makers still use centuries-old soap-making techniques.

STRAW MARQUETRY

Atelier Lison de Caunes
20—22 rue Mayet, 6th
01 40 56 02 10
www.lisondecaunes.com

Straw marquetry, a fragile and painstaking craft, is the specialty of Lison de Caunes and her assistants. Madame de Caunes, the granddaughter of a famous *décorateur* of the 1920s, Andre Groult, works almost exclusively on commission from her modest atelier. She employs straw just as wood is used to devise delicate marquetry patterns on furniture, boxes, lamps, mirrors, and room screens.

INVALIDES AND THE EIFFEL TOWER:

7th arrondissement

This is my old neighborhood, and I adore it. The produce and cheese market on the rue Cler is one of the city's best, and the main shopping streets of the 7th arrondissement house some of Paris's most esteemed makers of specialty goods and surprising finds.

ARMAGNAC

Ryst-Dupeyron
79 rue du Bac, 7th
01 45 48 80 93
www.dupeyron.com

The Paris showroom of one of France's most beloved spirits producers, made in the southwest (chapter 5), enjoys a prestigious address and decor to match. Come here for the ambience, as well as for professional guidance on purchasing from their impressive collection of Armagnacs and Bordeaux wines.

CORK PRODUCTS

Au Liegeur
17 avenue de la Motte Picquet, 7th
01 47 05 53 10
www.au-liegeur.com

Au Liegeur spins a million little objects from cork in its family-run factory in Soustons, in the Landes region of southwestern France. The Paris boutique shows off a fascinating array of specialty stoppers for wine, champagne, and liqueur bottles, as well as desk accessories and sheets of cork to cover floors and walls.

FRAMES

Atelier du Bois Doré
18 rue de Beaune, 7th
01 40 20 05 74

Period-style picture frames, sconces, decorative objects, and other indescribably ornate articles glitter against the dark walls of the Atelier du Bois Doré. This is considered one of the city's best creators and restorers of gilded wood, and a great place for a typically Parisian souvenir.

FURNITURE

François Hayem
13 rue du Bac, 7th
01 42 61 25 60

These are not reproductions. This luxurious gallery displays choice pieces of eighteenth- and nineteenth-century French furniture in styles from Louis Philippe to Napoleon III. François Hayem is one of the country's most recognized experts on French antique furniture, and can provide you with more information than you dreamed possible. Expect to pay several thousand euros for a museum-quality piece.

*Moissonnier
28 rue du Bac, 7th
01 42 61 84 88
52 rue de l'Universite, 7th
01 92 61 84 88
www.moissonnier.com

Of all the furniture makers in Paris, Moissonnier is one of my favorites, mostly for its modern twists on classic period styles. Moissonnier does more with red and black than anyone I've ever seen, and it's this knack for color and form that has earned it a reputation in the design trade. Moissonnier's artisans begin with inspiration from traditional French pieces—eighteenth-century commodes, Louis XVI *fauteuils*—but end with whimsical and dramatic pieces that are very now. I fell for a black chest with gold star pulls, but you can also have them custom design a piece with your choice of wood and fabric. Headquartered in Bourg-en-Bresse, there is a small atelier in the back of the rue du Bac location.

JEWELRY

Jacques Mazet
79 rue du Bac, 7th
01 45 48 60 58
www.mazetparis.com

Next door to Ryst-Dupeyron, in an elegant building faced with wood, sits one of the quarter's most well-regarded artisanal jewelers, Jacques Mazet. Mazet's traditional gemstone rings, necklaces, and bracelets—all made in this unassuming workshop—are jaw-droppingly lovely. Mazet will create a drawing of a custom piece for you, and in some cases will even make a model before handcrafting the final piece. Expect to pay 1,000 to 4,000 euros for off-the-shelf baubles, and more for custom work.

PERFUME AND GLOVES

Frédéric Malle
37 rue de Grenelle, 7th
01 42 22 76 40
www.editionsdeparfums.com

See listing, page 45.

Maître Parfumeur et Gantier
84 bis rue de Grenelle, 7th
01 45 44 61 57
www.maitre-parfumeur-et-gantier.com

In the eighteenth century, *grandes dames* purchased their gloves and their perfume at the same place; in fact, the two industries were linked initially (chapter 6). Today, Jean Laporte, former proprietor of the successful L'Artisan Parfumeur enterprise, brings the concept of *parfumeur-et-gantier* back to life in Paris, where there were once several hundred of these enterprises. The gloves sold in this shop are handmade in Millau, a town in central France known for this craft (chapter 5). The gloves are scented with a special process using microgranules of perfume, so that the fragrance remains in the glove for a long time. House scents start at 75 euros, or you can spend less on a terra-cotta box filled with fragrance for a room or drawer.

P. de Nicolai
80 rue de Grenelle, 7th
01 45 44 59 59
www.pnicolai.com

See listing, page 45.

PORCELAIN AND FAIENCE

*Le Cabinet d'Amateur
2 rue des Saints-Pères, 7th
01 42 60 60 00

As a ceramics lover, this is my own personal fantasy land. In a hushed, dim gallery, dramatically lit pieces of museum-quality faience and porcelain from Sèvres, Marseille, Nevers, and Italian centers like Deruta and Castelli, all dating from the sixteenth to the eighteenth centuries, are displayed like sparkling gems. This is one of France's most respected dealers of antique faience and porcelain. If you can afford it, you won't find a more choice selection.

Lefèbvre et Fils
24 rue du Bac, 7th
01 42 61 18 40

Behind a chic exterior stands one of Paris's best dealers of fine antique ceramics. Founded in 1880, the Lefèbvre family has a knack for finding unique Parisian pieces. On one of my visits, they had amassed an important collection of nineteenth-century tableware decorated with the monuments of Paris—a precursor to today's tourist trinkets sold along the rue de Rivoli.

RUGS

Manufacture des Tapis de Cogolin
42 rue de Bourgogne, 7th
01 40 62 77 00
www.manufacture-cogolin.com

This is the Paris showroom of the French Riviera's exclusive maker of custom rugs (chapter 6). If you have a movie-star budget and equally grand ideas for your interior decor, this is the place to go for a cotton or wool rug that is truly one-of-a-kind.

TABLE LINENS

Dominique Cartier
29 rue de Bourgogne, 7th
01 45 50 44 75

After working as a stylist and designer for Christofle and Lanvin, Dominique Cartier set up her own shop specializing in custom table linens. Starting with a color, idea, sketch, or swatch, she will design custom curtains, napkins, tablecloths, or other pieces in linen, cotton, or satin.

TAPESTRIES

*Galerie Robert Four
8 rue Saints Pères, 7th
01 40 20 44 96
www.aubusson-manufacture.com

One of the city's chicest streets for antiques shopping houses the Paris showroom of Robert Four, a well-regarded traditional tapestry maker from Aubusson in the Limousin region (chapter 4). This showroom is a museum of sorts, showcasing not only new creations but also restored antique tapestries, as well as *cartons*, the painted "sketches" created in the process of tapestry design. This is a terrific place to come for a crash course in tapestry. Watch a video that describes the process, giving you a feel for the atmosphere in the Aubusson factory, which employs some two dozen weavers working at giant looms. You can spend as little as a few hundred euros for a pillow, or up to many thousands for an antique or reproduction tapestry.

UMBRELLAS AND CANES

Madeleine Gély
218 boulevard Saint-Germain, 7th
01 42 22 17 06

A trip to Madeleine Gély is a walk back in time, when umbrellas and canes were handmade on-site to serve the needs of each customer. A mind-boggling array of antique and new umbrellas and canes lures curious passersby into this historic shop, open in this location since 1834. An evocative rustic walking stick from the mountainous region of the Auvergne won my heart. Don't miss the atelier next door, where you can watch artisans crafting umbrellas—"no plastic!" they emphasize—selling for 100 euros and up. You can choose a handle, then have them trim your parasol with everything from crystals to mink (yes, mink). Madame Gély even offers a lifetime guarantee. Former President François Mitterrand figures among a loyal customer base in France and abroad.

SOUTHERN PARIS:

13th, 14th, and 15th arrondissements

Tourist attractions, as well as interesting shopping opportunities, lie fewer and farther between in the 13th, 14th, and 15th arrondissements. Nonetheless, the area is home to two "biggies" of Parisian craft history: the Gobelins tapestry *manufacture* and the bustling flea market at the Porte de Vanves.

ANTIQUES AND FLEA MARKETS

*Porte de Vanves
Avenue Marc Sangnier and Avenue Georges Lafenestre, 14th

This is my favorite of the city's great weekend antiques markets. I have spied treasures here ranging from marble and bronze mantle decorations to chandeliers, lace parasols, quality copperware, and old skeleton keys. Market hours are Saturday and Sunday, 9:00 A.M. to dusk.

MONASTIC CRAFTS

Boutique de l'Artisanat Monastique
68 bis avenue Denfert-Rochereau, 14th
01 43 35 15 76
www.artisanat-monastique.com

This two-level extravaganza sells goods hand-crafted by monks and nuns from all over France. On one wall of the store, a map with thumbtacks shows where everything originates, from jams and jellies to cookies, soaps, lotions, linens, tableware, toys, and even lacy nightgowns—*mon Dieu!*

TAPESTRIES

Manufacture Nationale des Gobelins
42 avenue des Gobelins, 13th
01 44 61 21 69
www.manufacturedesgobelins.fr

In the mid-fifteenth century, Jean and Philibert Gobelin, brothers in a family of prosperous fabric dyers, set up shop along the Bièvre, a stream running through the outskirts of Paris. Their business gained a reputation as one of the best in the kingdom, and in the 1660s, Louis XIV's finance minister, Jean-Baptiste Colbert, tapped the Gobelins's company as a royal tapestry and furniture maker. From the 1690s, the company focused exclusively on magnificent tapestries for wall hangings and upholstery, which now adorn many state buildings and châteaux. In the museum, you can appreciate the techniques of tapestry making, which have remained essentially unchanged since the seventeenth century.

VARIOUS CRAFTS

Un Jour Un Artisan
23/31 bis rue Violet, 15th
01 45 79 33 91

This innovative gallery highlights a different artisan each day. Usually, the craftsperson is on-site to share his trade with visitors. Call ahead to find out when to see Renato Boaretto, a charming Venetian-born maker of *automates*, or handmade mechanical toys. Boaretto comes from his home studio in Mareil-en-France to demonstrate his music boxes, as well as porcelain, silk-clad puppets whose movements are perfectly choreographed.

PARIS OUTSKIRTS

Over the centuries, some of France's best-known creators of handmade luxuries have gotten their start on the outskirts of Paris, where they toiled in the service of the king and other French nobility. Today, many of these historic enterprises continue important craft traditions.

CHANTILLY

LACE

Musée du Patrimoine et de la Dentelle
34 rue d'Aumale
03 44 58 28 44

Black lace from Chantilly was all the rage among fashion-conscious European women during the eighteenth century. From parasols to shawls, overlays for balloon-shaped skirts and elaborate headdresses, *grenadine d'Alais*, as it was known, was immediately recognizable because of its characteristic hexagonal stitch made with long spindles. The municipal museum of Chantilly, north of Paris, is the only place to view examples of this fancy finery, which once employed some four thousand artisans, but alas, is no longer made. Antique examples of this fragile craft are rare, but sometimes turn up in local antiques markets.

TOILE DE JOUY

Musée de la Toile de Jouy
54 rue Charles de Gaulle
01 39 56 48 64

Jouy-en-Josas, south of Paris, is home to a relatively new museum devoted to *toile de Jouy*,

the ubiquitous and classic French fabric decorated with scenes of pastoral perfection, complete with happy peasants and delightful countrysides. The museum traces the story of the old Oberkampf *manufacture* (see page 28), the enterprise that popularized these fabrics, which have enjoyed a surprisingly long life. The museum offers easily transportable gifts printed in toile patterns—a very French souvenir.

SAINT-DENIS

SILVER

Bouilhet-Christofle Musée
112 rue Ambroise-Croizat
01 49 22 41 15
www.christofle.com

Christofle, one of France's most revered silver companies, leads visitors through more than a century and a half of silversmithing at its museum in Saint-Denis, north of Paris. Still producing luxurious table settings in its nineteenth-century factory, the company displays some two thousand of its best pieces of silver, and you can witness silversmithing techniques. The boutique carries a limited selection of small gifts; for the complete collection, head to the rue Royale showroom (page 46).

SAINT-OUEN

ANTIQUES AND FLEA MARKETS

Porte de Clignancourt
93400 Saint-Ouen

The Saint Ouen/Porte de Clignancourt market (locals call it simply *les puces*) is the largest flea market in Paris, and one of the oldest, with more than two centuries of history behind it. Any given Saturday or Sunday you might score vintage Baccarat, a bronze chandelier, or a charming old-world clock waiting for a tune-up. The neighborhood, technically in Saint-Ouen but bordering Paris's northernmost 18th arrondissement, is seedy, so stuff a credit card and a little cash in your pocket, leave your valuables at home, and enjoy.

SÈVRES

PORCELAIN

*Manufacture Nationale de Sèvres
Place de la Manufacture
01 46 29 22 06
www.manufacturedesevres.culture.gouv.fr

Because it remains government owned, the facilities and grounds of the Sèvres porcelain works could not be grander. The *manufacture*, founded in 1740, produces some five thousand pieces annually, most destined for state purposes and embassies. If you want to visit this extraordinary example of French artisanal patrimony, call in advance to arrange a tour. If instead you want to buy, you're better off hitting the official Paris Sèvres showroom (page 40), or combing the city's antiques shops specializing in ceramic wares.

BELGIUM

LUXEMBOURG

GERMANY

• Longwy

LORRAINE

Sarreguemines •

Saint-Louis-lès-Bitche •

Betschdorf
•

CHAMPAGNE–ARDENNE

• Nancy
• Vannes-le-Châtel

Soufflenheim •

• Lunéville

Baccarat •

Strasbourg •

ALSACE
Muttersholtz
•

• Bayel

• Mirecourt

• Ribeauvillé

Gérardmer •

SWITZERLAND

Chapter 2:

NORTHEASTERN FRANCE

B ordering Belgium, Luxembourg, Germany, and Switzerland, north-eastern France bears the mark of many cultural influences. Alsace-Lorraine enjoys the distinction of making some of France's most famous hand-wrought items: the magnificent crystal of Baccarat and Daum. Yet this region boasts lesser-known traditions with even longer legacies, including the modest pottery of Betschdorf and Soufflenheim, and table linens from Ribeauvillé, not to mention lace and violins from Mirecourt.

Alsace and parts of Lorraine have bounced back and forth between German and French rule since the tenth century; these two northeasternmost regions officially became part of France, in the latest territorial squabble, only at the end of World War II. Indeed this is France, but with a distinctly German accent. Many residents have German-sounding names, and the traditional costumes and architecture share more in common with Munich than Paris. You will even hear Alsatian, the local dialect, spoken in the shops of Strasbourg and villages surrounding it. The mountains are filled with wood-carvers and clock makers, and home cooks churn out gingerbread.

Champagne-Ardenne, bordering Lorraine to the west, always has stood firmly within the French realm, and is of course famous for the bubbly drink that bears its name. However, the region also boasts one of the oldest and most prestigious crystal factories in France at Saint-Louis-les-Bitche. It also houses one of the last villages known for basket weaving, once one of France's most prolific industries.

THE TRADITIONS

ALSATIAN POTTERY

Poterie Alsatienne

T wo tiny towns—Betschdorf and Soufflenheim, both north of Strasbourg— perpetuate the centuries-old tradition of Alsatian pottery. Utilitarian wares—plates, pitchers, wine jugs, tankards, and cowbells—that emerge from local shops exude a rustic style that epitomizes French country spirit.

Red clay has been pulled from the forest of Hagenau since prehistoric times, and potters are documented in Soufflenheim and Betschdorf, about six miles apart, as far back as the Middle Ages. In the 1700s, potters there invented a novel technique of firing hand-turned pottery at higher-than-average temperatures, and adding salt toward the end of the firing process. People valued the resulting pieces for their remarkable durability and water-resistance, as well as for the beautiful transparent quality of the glaze.

In Betschdorf, a town of a mere three thousand residents clustered within quaint timber-framed houses, a dozen or so potters keep the tradition alive. A few of the families—including Schmitter and Remmy (see the listings)—trace their pottery heritage back several centuries. Today classic Betschdorf wares bear a *gris et bleu* color scheme, a grey glaze with bright cobalt blue decoration including fruit, leaves, and geometrical motifs, some highlighted with engraving.

Soufflenheim upholds its own pottery tradition, more ornate and colorful, but still based on utilitarian stoneware—plates, pitchers, terrines, casseroles, and other vessels that radiate country charm. Typical wares include molds for *kouglof* (or *kougel-hopf*), a sweet brioche with almonds and raisins that Alsatians eat for breakfast or dessert, or as snacks. The distinctive swirled form of this delectable treat comes from the ceramic molds that the region's potters craft. Other ceramic molds in the form of hearts, pinwheels, and similar folk designs are used for making special cakes. Typical motifs on other vessels include geese, storks, doves, fruit and vegetal designs, and flowers and wheat. At the beginning of the nineteenth century, Soufflenheim's pottery studios employed some six hundred people. Today, a mere twenty pottery firms in Soufflenheim carry on this tradition.

In addition to this humble tradition of pottery, northeastern France was once home to more refined, decorative faience. These pieces were characterized by fussy floral decoration against a white background, and sometimes frilly, openwork edges. The faience tradition is more recent, getting started in the 1700s in Lunéville, Sarreguemines, and Strasbourg. With a few exceptions, faience is no longer artisanally produced in northeastern France. Sarreguemines evolved into an industrial ceramics center, producing washbasins, toilets, and tile, and the Lunéville factory turns out a limited production of tableware. The best bet for finding quality Alsatian faience is to scout some of the excellent antique stores in Strasbourg for an old piece.

L'ORIGINAL

The quality of Alsatian pottery can be hit or miss, as some designs are actually silkscreened rather than hand-painted. In Soufflenheim, the *Confrerie des Artisans Potiers de Soufflenheim* has developed a trademark to help consumers recognize wares crafted using traditional methods and styles. The trademark is a pair of hands interlocked around a bowl, in a medieval style.

ÇA COUTE COMBIEN?

Pottery from Betschdorf and Soufflenheim is valued for culinary use, as the high temperatures used in the firing process make it suitable for the oven and microwave. These pieces are relative bargains, with a vast selection between 10 and 50 euros.

CRÈME DE LA CRÈME

Visit Michel Streissel's studio in Soufflenheim (page 73), as much for the ceramics as for the delicious freshly cooked quiche he makes in his pottery studio.

CRYSTAL AND GLASS

Cristal et verre

Baccarat and Daum, France's top names in crystal and glass, have put the region of Lorraine on the map.

Baccarat's history stretches back to the 1760s, when the bishop of Metz founded a glassworks called Verrerie de Sainte-Anne-de-Baccarat, establishing a viable industry for an otherwise poor village. The location was chosen for the nearby forest, which supplied wood to fire the great furnaces needed to produce glass. Originally, the establishment made simple utilitarian objects including tableware, bottles, and window glass.

Through the beginning of the nineteenth century, the glassworks underwent several changes in name and ownership, but it survived the upheavals of the French Revolution and the Napoleonic Wars. In 1816, it began creating crystal by adding lead to the glass recipe. By 1822, a new group of owners had renamed the *manufacture* Compagnie de Cristalleries de Baccarat, with a focus on high-quality crystal that remains its cornerstone today. By the mid-nineteenth century, Baccarat had gained a reputation as the "crystal of kings," and it graced the tables of heads of state around the globe, from Russian czars to German chancellors, Saudi Arabian prices, Turkish sultans, and American presidents.

Baccarat crystal is still made the same way it has been for some two centuries. The production process begins with fine sand (which constitutes about 60 percent of the final product) and a few other ingredients—much the same as glass—except that lead (about 30 percent of the final product) is added. It's the lead that

accounts for crystal's most valued features—its bell-like tone when touched, its heft and sparkling brilliance, and its ability to refract light. Today, one-fifth of the residents of Baccarat work in the crystal factory.

The first artisan to touch a piece of lead crystal is the gaffer; his job is to scoop up a blob of the molten sand/lead mixture with the end of a blowpipe, then twist the pipe and blow into it, then pull the vessel and cut it over an open flame. During the process, the piece needs to be reheated over an extremely hot chamber called a gloryhole. Copper, cobalt, or maganese may be added to the mixture to create colored crystal. The gaffer continues to work on the piece as it takes its final form—a goblet, a glass, or a vase. To form certain shapes and add spouts, handles, or other ornamentation, artisans use special metal tools forged by a blacksmith, the design of which has remained virtually unchanged for centuries.

Fashions have waxed and waned in Baccarat crystal. In the nineteenth century, millefiori paperweights (created with colored glass rods, imitating Venetian styles) were popular. Later, colored goblets in amber and red came into vogue. Today, however, devoted wine drinkers accept nothing but colorless crystal, so that they can inspect the hue of their wine.

Daum is another glassmaking legend from Lorraine, based in Nancy. In 1878, brothers Auguste and Antonin Daum left established careers as an attorney and engineer to take over a glassworks their father had purchased. The brothers quickly became known for their colored lamps, many in the shape of mushrooms and flowers, with wrought-iron bases. Daum's real claim to fame, though, is bringing Art Nouveau style to life in glass, with its characteristic natural forms of flowers, grass, leaves, undulating plants, and scrolls.

Daum also pioneered the technique of *pâte de verre*, or glass paste, which imparts a lovely translucent finish to its pieces and allows for subtle coloration and patterns, such as flowers or swirls, in relief across the surface of a vessel. *Pâte de verre* begins with powdered glass and coloring agents, which is mixed into a gooey paste and then poured into a mold. The artisans at Daum add lead to the mixture, making it closer to crystal. The mold goes into a kiln, where the *pâte de verre* melts into its intricately carved designs, resulting in a relief pattern once the piece has cooled. This technique, although known since ancient Egypt, was refined by French artisans in the late nineteenth and early twentieth centuries; today, the Daum glassworks is still considered one of the masters of *pâte de verre*.

Similar to the heritage of Daum, the products of another Alsatian glassworks, Lalique, have enjoyed a lasting vogue around the world with their Art Nouveau and Art Deco styles. René Lalique (1860–1945) began his career as a jeweler, creating designs for famous Paris jewelry houses including Cartier and Boucheron. Later, he turned to designing art glass, and the company that bears his name, though an internationally known luxury brand, remains true to the spirit and style of the works crafted by its founder. Lalique's creations are, like Daum's, made primarily with *pâte de verre*, but the production focuses on more figural and sculptural works rather than housewares.

Saint-Louis-les-Bitche, in Champagne, is another lesser-known yet high-quality glassworks. Saint-Louis holds the distinction of being the oldest continuously producing crystal house in France. Founded in 1586, it became a royal glass works in 1767. Its crystal has graced tables from Versailles to Istanbul. In the 1990s, the company became associated with the luxury group Hermès, which has brought it even greater cachet.

Among the production of these renowned crystal makers, perfume bottles hold a particular place of honor. In the early nineteenth century apothecaries across France dispensed lavender water and eau de toilette in cut-glass containers for a lady's dressing table; some of these vessels were created by Baccarat, Daum, Saint-Louis, and Lalique. Today, crystal perfume bottles from the nineteenth and early twentieth centuries—some handmade for couture houses such as Chanel, Guerlain, and Dior—have become an obsession among collectors.

L'ORIGINAL

There is no such thing as seconds in Baccarat crystal. Daum, on the other hand, offers seconds, many still very high quality, at its outlets in Nancy and Vannes-le-Châtel.

ÇA COUTE COMBIEN?

At one of the Baccarat showrooms in France (or around the world), you can spend anywhere from 50 euros for a simple goblet to thousands of euros for an original crystal sculpture. There is a vigorous trade in antique Baccarat objects from the nineteenth and early twentieth centuries, with paperweights, flasks, and vases fetching up to tens of thousands of euros at auction.

CRÈME DE LA CRÈME

Though you can buy this esteemed crystal all over the world, visits to the factory stores of Baccarat (page 76) and Daum (page 78) offer an incomparable shopping experience.

LONGWY ENAMELS

Emaux de Longwy

Longwy, in northern Lorraine near the Belgian border, is home to sumptuous ceramic wares decorated with a type of cloisonné enamel that is unique in France, if not the world. The term *cloisonné* means compartmentalized, referring to discrete sections of rich color. We usually think of cloisonné as a jewelry-maker's technique; a jeweler creates a "skeleton" using bronze, gold, or silver strips or wires, then fills each compartment with molten enamel to achieve bright colors and a bold design in pendants, beads, and other pieces.

The peculiarity of Longwy is that its faience artisans, or *faïenciers,* apply the cloisonné technique to ceramics rather than metal. The technique was already known in Japan and other parts of Asia, but it was uncommon in Europe because the process is extremely laborious. However, the popularity of Asian ceramics inspired Longwy artisans to first accomplish this painstaking technical feat in the eighteenth century.

In 1798, Charles Régnier founded a *faïencerie,* or establishment for making faience, in Longwy-Bas, the lower part of town. In the 1820s, its artisans began creating the beautifully saturated enamels, including a full range of blues from royal to turquoise and the now-characteristic *bleu de Longwy.*

The *faïencerie's* artisans experimented with an enamel technique of applying a white, opaque glaze that allowed them to carve designs in relief on the surface of a vessel, imitating cloisonné compartments separated by metal. By the end of the century, they had refined the technique by creating carved relief and at the same time imparting a slick, reflective quality to the entire surface that was quickly celebrated by collectors. The pieces underwent several firings in the kiln, as well as an extensive finishing process.

Unfortunately, the original *faïencerie* that made Longwy famous declined and finally closed in the 1970s. Thankfully, however, a handful of ceramics masters carry on the peculiar tradition of Longwy enamels, including men who were initially associated with the original Faïencerie de Longwy.

L'ORIGINAL
Collectors value pieces of Longwy enamel for their characteristic *bleu de Longwy*, a lovely not-quite-turquoise shade, as well as the finely crackled effect of enamel across the surface.

ÇA COUTE COMBIEN?
You may be surprised by the steep prices of Longwy enamels—often several hundred euros for a plate or vase—which is the result of the intensive labor involved in producing these wares.

CRÈME DE LA CRÈME
The shop of Christian Leclercq, Emaux d'Art de Longwy, (page 77) is a great place to find an old or new Longwy piece.

TABLE LINENS

Linge de table

 iven the prominence of northeastern France in *les arts de la table*, is it any wonder that the region is known for its fabulous table linens?

Hand-stitched house linens have a humble yet enduring past in Alsace-Lorraine. These quality homespun tablecloths, napkins, bedspreads, pillowcases, and other utilitarian pieces are now popular among collectors for their French country charm. One of the most traditional types of linen from the region is *kelsch*, a bedcover or tablecloth patterned with squares in red and white, or blue and white. The term *kelsch* refers to the plant harvested to produce the intensely colored dyes used to create these fabrics; it was one of the main crops of northeastern France and Germany as far back as the Middle Ages. Eventually, *kelsch* came to describe the fabrics themselves.

Kelsch fabrics typify French country style, with their checkerboard patterns and bright colors. Making house linens was once a primary domestic activity during cold winters; women wove them on small looms in their homes. To make a warm bedcover, they stitched a hemp cloth lining on the bottom of a piece, then stuffed it with feathers or cotton. Only a few artisans today follow the true handmade techniques of creating *kelsch*, though machine-made imitations abound in shops across the region. The best place to see original *kelsch* fabrics is in the regional textile museums and antiques shops.

Though *kelsch* and other humble country fabrics endured over the years, by the seventeenth century some able weavers in the region had turned to producing fancier linens to meet the demand of the burgeoning nobility. Several artisanal enterprises distinguished themselves for their ability to print on fabric (and paper) using carved woodblocks, one for each color (the esteemed wallpaper company, Zuber, was founded in the area). In 1759, Louis XV granted one of the best, the Manufacture d'Impression sur Etoffes in Ribeauvillé, the right to produce fabric for the French crown. Today, cotton, wool, and silk tablecloths manufactured by this same enterprise, under the Beauvillé trade name, remain some of France's finest and most coveted table linens. Several additional important table linen makers in the region, including Le Jacquard Français, have also distinguished themselves for their fine craftsmanship.

L'ORIGINAL
Nearly all of Alsace-Lorraine's fabric printers have supplanted the woodblock print method with screen printing. It's still a laborious manual process, though, as each screen represents one color, and artisans layer the screens by hand to create a multicolored design.

ÇA COUTE COMBIEN?
The cost of an antique *kelsch*, one of the traditional homemade linens of Alsace, can run surprisingly high. Expect to pay several hundred to several thousand euros for one, depending on its size and state of preservation.

CRÈME DE LA CRÈME
The Beauvillé linen outlet in Ribeauvillé (page 75) is worth the trek for good deals on some of France's fanciest table dressings.

THE LISTINGS

ALSACE

Bas-Rhin

BETSCHDORF

Traditional Alsatian pottery keeps this one-horse town on the map. Typical half-timbered houses, many slanting from years of settling, add charm to this tiny village of potters. All the best works can be found along the main street, whose name changes from rue des Potiers to Grande Rue, then to rue Docteur Deutsch as you pass through town.

POTTERY

Albert Greiner
68 rue Docteur Deutsch
03 88 54 56 57

At first glance, this drab shop/residence, with its blasé proprietors and incongruous array of ocean-themed paintings and sculpted busts, may seem unpromising. If you stick to the pottery, however, you might come away with some of Betschdorf's most interesting pieces. Albert Greiner has helped keep the old traditions of *grès au sel* alive in Betschdorf, crafting solid pieces of traditional Alsatian pottery from his workshop in nearby Beinheim. What sets these works apart are the intricate painted designs and coiled leaf patterns, with hints of yellow, brown, and green. This is one of Betschdorf's best values, as you will pay a fair price (just 15 to 70 euros) for some of the most traditional plates, mugs, and pitchers in town.

*Claude Schmitter
Corner of rue des Potiers and
    rue Saint-Jean
03 88 54 42 95

Michèle Weiss, granddaughter of Claude Schmitter, carries on her family's tradition of crafting historic Betschdorf pottery. Madame Weiss runs an efficient one-woman show, and you can watch her making lamps, vases, bells, and mugs in the traditional blue and gray, with the typical Betschdorf patterns and motifs—flowers, grapes, and checkerboard designs. She will modestly yet expertly explain the process to visitors who browse this happy conglomerate of house, atelier, and retail shop. A gamut of objects and prices—from 3 to 250 euros—means that there is something for every budget. This is hands-down Betschdorf's best value; for similar items in Strasbourg, you will pay double.

Musée de la Poterie
Museum Shop
2 rue de Kuhlendorf
03 88 54 48 07

Trace the history of Betschdorf pottery with a guided visit, audio tour, or video, and check out examples of vessels from the seventeenth through the nineteenth centuries. The shop sells a limited selection of quality wares at high prices. The museum collection is an excellent place to learn about the tradition and process of Betschdorf pottery, but when it's time to buy, hit the shops!

Poterie Remmy M.M.
16 rue des Potiers
03 88 54 49 38

Matthieu and Marlene Remmy—the "MM" of this one-oven operation—claim a ceramic heritage dating back to 1568, when the name Remmy was recorded in a local register as an Alsatian potter. Today, their selection is small, but the quality is high. In addition to traditional work, Madame Rémmy has designed a series of charming ceramic Alsatian women in local dress, some up to three feet tall. You can pay as little as 15 euros for a small pitcher, or up to 600 euros for one of the large Alsatian figurines.

*Poterie Remmy
8 rue Soufflenheim
03 88 54 44 16

Vincent Remmy runs this terrific shop on the outskirts of Betschdorf. Now in competition with his brother Matthieu (see above)—much to the admitted chagrin of their mother, who is also active in the trade—this branch of the Remmy ceramics family operates in a vast, airy, warehouselike space with the largest gamut of wares in Betschdorf. Family members walk around with clay on their hands, working on traditional pitchers and vessels, but also nativity scenes, figurines of saints, and strange tree sculptures, cranking out pottery from four ovens as if it were bread. Molded clay in all stages of production is displayed in multiple rooms. Prices run a bit higher than elsewhere in town, but you're guaranteed to walk away with something unique. This shop is located a quarter mile outside of town, but don't try to walk unless you're willing to brave speeding trucks. Reward yourself with an Alsatian beer or a *café* in the Remmy's small bar.

M U T T E R S H O L T Z

L I N E N S

Kelsch linens
Tissages Gander
2 rue de l'Étang
03 88 85 15 32

Michel Gander is one of the last artisans to produce *kelsch*, the traditional Alsatian checkerboard linens, using hand looms exclusively. The Gander family has been making these country linens since 1660. The shop opens for a few hours in the afternoon to sell simple and beautifully made tablecloths, curtains, bed linens, and lampshades, or fabric by the meter.

S O U F F L E N H E I M

Most of the potters' shops are located along a single main street—known along different lengths as Grande Rue, Mont de l'Eglise, then the rue Haguenau—which runs from the lower town to the higher part of Soufflenheim. Locals speak Alsatian (beware not to call it German, though it sounds similar) and the dress and ambience are distinctly Germanic. This is a great place to see artisans in action, as the friendly people of Soufflenheim are happy to show visitors around their workshops.

P O T T E R Y

Poterie Artisanale G Wehrling et Fille
64 rue Haguenau
03 88 86 65 25

This father-and-daughter enterprise is one of the most reputable in town. The picturesque shop with a red-tiled roof is packed to the brim with jars, pitchers, dishes, and religious objects painted with designs in brick red, ochre, and white. You can commission a special piece to celebrate a wedding or birth, inscribed with the name of the couple or new baby. These are good values considering the quality; you can pick up a nice vessel for under 50 euros.

Poterie Richard Hausswirth
1 rue Montée
03 88 86 74 31
www.alsace-poterie.com

Prominently situated at Soufflenheim's main intersection, the team of veteran potters at Poterie Hausswirth churns out the rustic tableware that has put this town on the map. The specialty here is bird motifs—swans, doves, and storks—which flit and land on plates, terrines, and the classic *kugelhopf* molds that characterize Soufflenheim style.

*Poterie Michel Streissel
25 rue Haguenau
03 88 86 64 69
www.streissel.com

Michel Streissel, a brawny, soft-spoken gentleman with a large mustache, is president of the brotherhood, or *confrerie*, of Soufflenheim potters, and he is passionate about his trade. Streissel completed the construction of a historically correct, wood-fired kiln in 2000, and you can witness his stoneware being fired several times a day. In the adjoining demonstration kitchen, the aroma of freshly baked quiche—cooked inside one of Streissel's casserole dishes, of course—welcomes visitors to this warm shop. Expect to pay more for the high-quality wares here, but rest assured that you can't buy more traditional designs than this.

Poterie Ludwig
5 rue des Potiers
03 88 86 60 24

Michel Ludwig's large workshop is chockful of brightly colored tableware displayed on red-and-white checked tablecloths that make you feel as though you've just stepped into a French country restaurant. This fourth-generation potter works alongside his wife and son, plus several assistants. He also takes on apprentices to make sure the torch of tradition is passed to the next generation. These industrious artisans churn out everything on the premises, and some of their work is sent to Strasbourg for resale in the city's boutiques. Prices are competitive: a small dessert bowl goes for as little as 4 euros, while a large terrine will set you back about 70 euros.

*Poterie Friedmann
3 rue Haguenau
03 88 86 61 21
www.poteriefriedmann.fr

The Friedmann family traces its artisanal roots back to 1802, when the first family member began baking clay in Soufflenheim. The workshop, retail space, and adjacent house and driveway serve as a memorial to this family history, with a large heart-shaped ceramic plaque featuring the family tree decorating one wall. This is a great place to observe the production process, as the workshop is completely open to visitors.

STRASBOURG

Picture-perfect Strasbourg is a great antiques-and-crystal shopping destination, with a nice balance of big-name and mom-and-pop stores.

CRYSTAL

Baccarat Boutique
44 rue Hallebardes
03 88 32 32 10
www.baccarat.fr

The style of the Strasbourg Baccarat storefront is unmistakable, and the interior as elegant as the few carefully lit items on display. You can spend as little as 100 euros for a set of wine glasses, or up to 15,000 euros for an extraordinary chandelier.

Daum Boutique
30 rue Mésange
03 88 21 95 18
www.daum.fr

Next door to Bernardaud, the Strasbourg showroom of the Daum crystal dynasty glimmers. The small, understated boutique sells lovely jewelry for less than 200 euros, or you can drop up to 3,000 euros on figurines of a giraffe or puma. The staff is appropriately snooty for this big-name house.

POTTERY

Poterie d'Alsace
3 rue Frères
03 88 32 23 21

If you don't have a chance to visit the regional pottery centers of Betschdorf or Soufflenheim, this is a good place to purchase rustic local wares. Traditional Alsatian cake molds, terrines, and other dishware abound in distinctive styles and colors. It's easy to miss the nearly closet-size shop; look for the dark green façade and sign.

TABLE LINENS

Nappes d'Alsace
6 rue Mercière
03 88 22 69 29

If you missed the Beauvillé linen outlet (following page), this is a good spot to purchase the famous Alsatian linens that grace well-appointed tables across France. Every square inch of this one-room shop is covered with *nappes*, or tablecloths, of every color and pattern, which the matronly proprietors will happily display for you. You can pick up an adorable baby bib for as few as 5 euros, or spend up to 250 euros for a large tablecloth. The shop is located along the heavily trafficked pedestrian street that leads to Strasbourg cathedral.

VARIOUS CRAFTS

*Arts et Collections d'Alsace
4 place du Marché aux Poissons
03 88 14 03 77

If you don't have time to visit all the villages of the Alsatian countryside, this is an excellent one-stop-shopping destination for high-quality crafts from the region. Alsatian linens are a specialty, beautifully displayed in an exclusive area of this large retail space. It also carries pottery from Betschdorf and Soufflenheim, wooden and metal toys, as well as blown glass and crystal. Prices range from 10 to 300 euros. The helpful staff can tell you more about your purchases, and elegantly box or bag them. The shop is located two blocks from the cathedral, but this is no tourist trap: it's the real deal.

Bastian et Fils
22–24 place de la Cathédrale
03 88 32 45 93

The store's windows reflect the Gothic flying buttresses of Strasbourg cathedral, providing a feast for the eyes outside as well as within. The smell of antique wood impregnates the air of this antiques dealer's stately store specializing in a range of the region's crafts—a full eighteenth-century dinner service, vintage tureens from Betschdorf and Soufflenheim, antique copper *kugelhopf* molds, beer steins, lithographs, ornate mirrors, handsome regional chairs and tables, and more goodies. You feel as though you've just walked into a well-furnished mansion, and as you explore the back rooms, the collections get better. Prices are commensurate with the quality in this treasure-trove of Alsatian craftsmanship.

Bernard Pfirsch
20 rue de la Nuée-Bleue
03 88 32 72 73

A treasure hunter's nirvana, every object in this antiques dealer's shop holds a story. Bernard and Janine Pfirsch, friendly and obsessive collectors of Alsatian crafts, have amassed a jumble of old Soufflenheim pottery, metal cake pans, farm implements, prints, linens, and a number of other objects. Old ceramic pots are piled so high they threaten to come crashing to the ground; there's no room for even one more *objet*. The creaky floor and stale aromas that waft from the space speak volumes about the history of

Alsace. You can spend as little as 5 euros for a crystal goblet, or shell out 500 for a set of mint-condition Alsatian ceramic terrines.

La Cour Renaissance
3 rue de l'Ail
03 88 52 01 21

Traditionally, Alsatian families presented couples with a wedding gift of furniture crafted in fir or pine and hand-painted with folkloric motifs. Antiques dealer Christine Demay has assembled a handpicked collection of these treasures—mostly armoires and chests—in her lovely boutique in the center of Strasbourg. The collection is rounded out by choice pieces of regional pottery and linens.

Musée Alsacien
23 quai Saint Nicolas
03 88 52 50 01

Although its shop is disappointing, this regional museum is worth visiting for the excellent collection of historical Alsatian pottery and furniture. You'll come away with a vision of life in preindustrial Alsace and understand why the craft trades were so vital to the society. The basement has a fun exhibition on the history of regional beer making.

Haut-Rhin

RIBEAUVILLÉ

LINENS

Beauvillé Magasin d'Usine
19 route de Sainte-Marie-aux-Mines
03 89 73 74 74
www.beauville.com

This is the official outlet store for Beauvillé, one of France's highest-quality brands of table linens. The spacious, unpretentious retail space displays its colorful linens on two floors. The staff is unusually customer focused, obliging questions by spreading out linens on a large table and pointing out special details. Prices depend on the number of colors in a piece—a measure of the labor involved. Expect to pay anywhere from 90 euros for a cloth with one or two colors and up to 300 euros for a multicolored piece—some 30 percent off French retail prices. Cushions, priced at 30 to 40 euros, are a particularly good deal. You need a car to reach this out-of-the-way store. Once there, you won't find any tourists, just knowledgeable buyers (mostly French) enjoying this excellent shopping experience.

CHAMPAGNE-ARDENNE

Aube

BAYEL

CRYSTAL

Cristallerie Royale de Champagne
La Voie Basse
03 25 92 37 60
www.bayel-cristal.com

The town of Bayel, in eastern Champagne, was already a glassmaking center in the Middle Ages. In a royal edict in 1666, Louis XIV authorized a Venetian glassmaker, Jean-Baptiste Mazzolay, to found a royal glassworks there. The Cristallerie Royale de Champagne began supplying the French court with sparkling tableware, and today it continues to provide collectors with beautiful goblets, decanters, candlestick holders, and other objects of thin crystal. Take one of the daily guided tours, where you can observe the artisans hand-blowing, cutting, sandblasting, and engraving decorative patterns. Some pieces are gilded or enameled to achieve remarkable coloration.

LORRAINE

Meurthe-et-Moselle

BACCARAT

The landscape around Baccarat is industrial and unimpressive, but it's worth the trek to bask in the glory of this world-renowned crystal house. Its museum and flagship store are the main attractions in town, along with a curious church with Baccarat crystal windows, Saint-Remy-de-Baccarat. Avoid the other shops in town, which sell lesser-quality wares; if you've come this far, buy the real thing.

CRYSTAL

Musée de Baccarat
20 rue des Cristalleries
03 83 76 61 37

Unfortunately, the factory isn't open to visitors, but you can still learn a lot at the Baccarat museum, housed in the former elegant residence of its factory managers. The museum lies behind the boutique, and is clearly marked. Here you can watch a video about the production process and view a small but impressive collection of crystal objects commissioned for heads of state.

Baccarat Boutique
2 rue des Cristalleries
03 83 76 60 01
www.baccarat.fr

The Baccarat boutique is located at the most important intersection of this eponymous town, and is impossible to miss with its trademark red-and-white decorative scheme. You might expect something more ornate or historic, but the digs couldn't be simpler— though still more elegant than your average factory store. This spacious, modern showroom, filled with light from windows on three walls, showcases tableware on one side, and decorative objects and jewelry on the other. The hushed, museumlike atmosphere invites you to focus your attention on the glistening array of wine glasses, pitchers, vases, champagne flutes, liqueur bottles, jewelry, and animal and cartoon figurines ranging from giraffes to Snoopy. You can spend as little as 60 euros for a simple wine goblet, or as much as 7,000 euros for an original sculpture that refracts light as you move around it. There's no such thing as seconds in Baccarat, as imperfect wares are smashed and melted down in the factory, but prices here are approximately 30 percent lower than in the United States.

LONGWY

Longwy, in northern Lorraine near the border with Belgium and Luxembourg, is divided into two parts—low and high. Lower Longwy (Longwy-Bas) boasts a small cluster of enamel artisans, but don't miss the ceramics museum in Upper Longwy (Longwy-Haut). What the town lacks in charm it makes up for in the stunning wares scattered among a few excellent enamelers.

ENAMELED FAIENCE

Emaux d'Art de Longwy
2 bis place Giraud
03 82 25 71 46

Christian Leclercq, winner of a prestigious Meilleur Ouvrier de France award for his cloisonné enamel wares, is one of the last artisans to have come from the now-defunct *faïencerie* that put Longwy on the map. This unpretentious shop alongside the bus depot in Longwy-Bas offers an excellent collection of antique pieces assembled under Leclercq's connoisseurial eye, as well as some of his own fine work. Prices are steep; you might pay 75 euros for a small faience dish, or up to 2,000 euros for a vase.

Emaux de Saintignon
6 avenue Saintignon
03 82 24 47 78

This is an excellent opportunity to see a good enamel craftsman at work, since Joel Barthélémy welcomes you into his atelier/store, where you can watch as he decorates a plate, pitcher, or vase. Barthélémy concentrates his efforts on special orders such as commemorative plates. Both the prices and quality are high, but the atmosphere is friendly and down-to-earth.

Faïencerie et Emaux de Longwy
3 rue des Emaux
03 82 24 30 94
www.emauxdelongwy.com

What appears from the exterior to be an unappealing modern shop in Longwy-Bas in fact offers some gorgeous historical reproductions. The artisans in this on-site workshop create pieces conceived by contemporary Longwy designers, but also produce copies of nineteenth- and twentieth-century museum pieces with Asian motifs. Prices are high; you will pay 150 euros for a small plate, or up to 3,000 for a lamp.

Château-Musée and Faïencerie Saint Jean l'Aigle
Château de la Faïencerie
Herserange/Longwy
03 82 24 58 20
www.emaux-de-longwy.com

This private ceramics museum in Longwy-Haut displays classic pieces from the eighteenth and nineteenth centuries, and is an excellent place to learn about the history and laborious process of enameling ceramic wares. You can watch artisans toiling in the adjacent workshop, and purchase some of their quality works.

LUNÉVILLE SAINT-CLÉMENT

Lunéville has two historical claims to fame: faience and pearled embroidery. Unfortunately, both of these once-vibrant craft traditions are now all but dead. Just two little enterprises keep the torch of tradition alive in this otherwise drab town.

EMBROIDERY

Conservatoire des Broderies de Lunéville
Château de Lunéville
03 83 73 56 86
www.broderie-lunéville.com

This happy find makes a trip to otherwise dreary Lunéville worthwhile. The sole conservator of a once-thriving industry, this private museum created by Françoise Remy traces the history of *lunévilleuses*, a term that still appears in the Larousse French dictionary meaning pearled or spangled embroidery. At the beginning of the twentieth century, some twenty-five thousand embroiderers worked at this craft, creating materials for flapper dresses and other glamorous fashions popular at the time around the globe. After World War II, only seven workshops remained. Part of the museum's mission is to pass on this tradition to the next generation. The boutique sells small examples of pearled embroidery, extraordinary in their beauty, for 20 to 40 euros. The museum is housed in the Château de Lunéville, a gargantuan castle that sought to emulate the grandeur and gardens of Versailles.

FAIENCE

Manufacture de Lunéville Saint-Clément
1 rue Keller et Guérin
03 83 74 07 58

Incongruously, Lunéville tableware with feminine, fussy floral designs adorns the shelves of one of the most generic factory stores in France. The windowless warehouse, flooded with garish fluorescent lighting, nonetheless offers endless shelves piled high with quality white and cream dishes, bowls, and cups. The upstairs "museum"—more of an extension of the factory store—includes a collection of vintage Lunéville faience and some historical photos. You will pay less here for Lunéville wares priced higher elsewhere: dinner plates start at 6 euros, a serving dish goes for 50, and expect to pay up to 400 for a lamp.

NANCY

Nancy is a gem of a city and a shopper's paradise. Plan to depart from Nancy with everything from fashion accessories to specialty food items, and of course, the brilliant crystal for which this lovely city is known. Classy and posh, with a taste for traditional, sophisticated style, this is a place to dress to impress, to see and be seen.

The Office de Tourisme, just off the main place Stanislas, has a small boutique of Nancy's signature crafts, but save your euros for the shops. Everything of interest is within close range in the city center, except for the Daum factory store, which you'll need to take a cab or the tram to reach.

CRYSTAL

Baccarat Boutique
2 rue Dominicains
03 83 30 55 11
www.baccarat.fr

Just off place Stanislas, the characteristic red façade and white awnings of the Baccarat boutique draw you in to peruse two large rooms full of its signature pieces. The staff is suitably snooty, especially toward curious tourists spilling over from the Office de Tourisme across the street.

Daum Boutique
14 place Stanislas
03 83 32 21 65
www.daum.fr

This Nancy institution occupies a privileged corner on place Stanislas, and it couldn't be more elegant. On three floors, showrooms display stunningly gorgeous crystal wares. The first floor carries Daum's latest collection, presented by smiling, knowledgeable, and attractive saleswomen. You will pay as little as 120

euros for a small dog or pendant, or as much as 2,000 euros for a larger sculptural piece. The second and third floors hold the works of artists who have designed pieces for Daum through the ages, including Salvador Dalí, who conceived both a strange prickly crystal snail as well as surrealist broken vases. Most pieces on the second and third floors do not carry price tags, for those with unlimited budgets.

Magasin d'Usine Daum
17 rue Cristalleries
03 83 32 14 55

The no-pressure staff makes perusing the light, airy showroom of the Daum factory store a pleasure. Here you can view an educational video about the process of designing and creating crystal, or linger in front of dinnerware and decorative objects. The atmosphere is chic yet relaxed. In addition to large-format and historical works for display only, you can purchase pieces such as a puma or goat figurine for 200 to 400 euros, a large vase for 1,200, or a serving dish for around 400 euros—some 30 to 40 percent below full retail price. The hulking factory, where artisans still rely on handmade techniques to form and finish the *pâte de verre* works, is unfortunately off-limits to visitors.

Moselle

SAINT-LOUIS-LÈS-BITCHE

CRYSTAL

*Cristalleries Saint-Louis
Rue Goetlosquet
03 87 06 40 04

The stunning vista of the historic crystal factory at Saint-Louis-lès-Bitche—nestled in the bottom of a verdant valley—is worth the descent on route D36A from Lemberg to this off-the-beaten-path destination. The gigantic, red-roofed crystalworks and the few homes snuggled up against it are all there is to this modest village. You can capture the entire scene in one snapshot from the height of the surrounding hills, often covered in fog that imparts a mysterious, quiet air.

The first glassworks in Lorraine, founded in 1586, began producing crystal in 1871 and is now owned by the luxury company Hermès. The factory shop has limited hours, and uncharacteristically for France closes at 5:00 P.M., so call ahead. You can find good deals on factory seconds of its distinctive, brightly colored crystal and other pieces discounted some 30 to 40 percent. Unfortunately, the factory is normally off-limits to the public except for prearranged group tours, and is strangely guarded by a slew of security guards and surrounded by a huge metal fence. A much-needed restoration to this historic giant of a building is underway. The posh Saint-Louis showroom in Paris (page 44) is certainly more accessible, but is nowhere near as interesting as visiting this odd little town.

SARREGUEMINES

Sarreguemines, with a pleasant downtown and a few pedestrian-only streets, quickly becomes industrial if you walk too far in any direction. The faience that made this town famous has not been produced in thirty years, and the local enterprises now mostly make building tiles. The so-called "factory store" in town sells "Sarreguemines faience" that is actually made in Lunéville and shipped here. Stick to the museum.

FAIENCE

Musée de la Faïence
17 rue Poincaré
03 87 98 93 50
www.sarreguemines-museum.com

This nice museum is a sad reminder of what was lost when the town's artisans stopped producing the beautiful colored wares that made the Sarreguemines *manufacture* a major player in the world of eighteenth-century faience. If you want to learn more, another museum in the northern section of town, Moulin de la Blies, demonstrates the steps involved in the faience-making process.

VANNES-LE-CHÂTEL

CRYSTAL

Magasin d'Usine Daum
Allamps / Highway D4
03 83 25 41 01

The famous Daum crystal is designed and made at the main factory in Nancy, but some pieces are manufactured, on a more industrial scale, as a series here in Vannes-le-Châtel. At the factory store, the stunning, colorful designs stand in stark contrast to the drab space, with its dull gray shelves and carpeting. Two large rooms display some lower-priced wares such as water and wine glasses in the 25-euro range, rings and pendants for 100 euros, and vases for up to 1,300 euros.

Vosges

GÉRARDMER

This quiet mountain town, with its fresh air and small ski resort, seems an unlikely setting for one of France's most prestigious producers of table linens, Le Jacquard Français.

LINENS

Le Jacquard Français
Boutique: 35 rue Charles de Gaulle
03 29 60 85 50
Factory store: 45 boulevard Kelsch
03 29 60 09 04
www.le-jacquard-francais.fr

The shelves of the plain, outletlike boutique are filled to the brim with the colorful table linens of this famous maker. Linens are arranged according to price, and the helpful shopkeepers will spread out individual napkins for 3 euros, or tablecloths that run between 50 and 150 euros. I love a recent collection with bright, crisp stripes in tangerine, fuschia, and lime. At the factory store, prices are the same as those at the boutique in town—approximately 30 percent off the full retail prices.

MIRECOURT

This attractive, bustling town is known for two unrelated craft traditions: lace and stringed instruments. Violin making was introduced to Mirecourt in the sixteenth century, and the town once counted some four hundred luthiers; today there are about ten. The good news is that esteemed luthier Etienne Vatelot has founded the National School of Luthiers in his hometown, and the institution is a magnet for would-be stringed instrument makers from around the world.

LACE

Maison de la Dentelle
Hôtel de Ville
1 bis Place Chantaire
03 29 37 39 59

The Maison de la Dentelle is the sole institution to carry on a once-vibrant lace-making tradition. Here you can observe women working at the painstakingly slow process of creating bobbin lace, *dentelle aux fuseaux*. Members of the local lace makers' association rotate through this space, keeping the torch of tradition alive, inch by inch. A few small pieces of lace are for sale in the attached store. Currently located on the second floor of the town hall or Hôtel de Ville, plans are in place to move the Maison de la Dentelle behind the tourist office.

STRINGED INSTRUMENTS

Anne-Sophie and Catherine Benoit
5 rue Saint Georges
03 29 37 00 98
www.atelier-baroin-benoit.fr

Anne-Sophie and Catherine Benoit are hard at work preserving antique violins and bows in the tiny workshop they opened together in 2000. Their specialty is restoring old violins, which they sell for around 2,000 euros. It's refreshing to see an artisan studio run by women, a relative rarity in Alsace-Lorraine.

**Musée de la Lutherie et Maison
du Violoncelle**
Cours Stanislas
03 29 37 81 59

A gigantic cello, some twenty-five feet tall, greets you in the main hall of this museum of stringed-instrument making. Organized around the central hall are smaller galleries displaying historic violins and memorabilia documenting the history of luthiers in Mirecourt. There is nothing to buy here, but through the museum and tourist office you can arrange visits to private luthier workshops not normally open to the public, where you can commission a one-of-a-kind instrument.

Roland Terrier
17 rue Chanzy
03 29 37 31 38
www.cognier-terrier.com

A museumlike display of violins and cellos—all handmade by Roland Terrier—hang along one wall of this neat-as-a-pin workshop. Friendly and talkative, Monsieur Terrier can show you how he crafts the shiny artisanal instruments that sell for 600 to 4,000 euros.

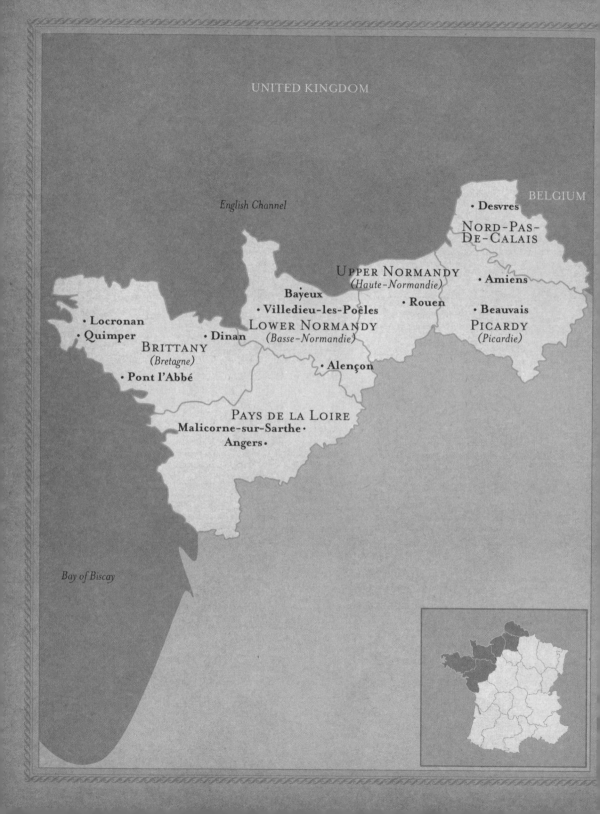

UNITED KINGDOM

BELGIUM

English Channel

• **Desvres**

Nᴏʀᴅ-Pᴀs-
Dᴇ-Cᴀʟᴀɪs

Uᴘᴘᴇʀ Nᴏʀᴍᴀɴᴅʏ
(Haute-Normandie)

• **Amiens**

• **Bayeux**
• **Villedieu-les-Poêles**
• **Rouen**

• **Beauvais**

Lᴏᴡᴇʀ Nᴏʀᴍᴀɴᴅʏ
(Basse-Normandie)

Pɪᴄᴀʀᴅʏ
(Picardie)

• **Locronan**
• **Quimper**
• **Dinan**

Bʀɪᴛᴛᴀɴʏ
(Bretagne)

• **Alençon**

• **Pont l'Abbé**

Pᴀʏs ᴅᴇ ʟᴀ Lᴏɪʀᴇ
Malicorne-sur-Sarthe •
Angers •

Bay of Biscay

Chapter 3

NORTHWESTERN FRANCE

❧

F rance's northwestern region, composed of Brittany, Upper and Lower Normandy, Nord-Pas-de-Calais, Picardy, and the Pays de La Loire, boasts what may be the country's richest history of textile arts, especially tapestry and lace. Home of the breathtaking eleventh-century Bayeux Tapestry, the region once counted an extraordinary number of female artisans making everything from lace costumes to tapestries, sailcloth, and fishing nets. Bayeux and Beauvais were important tapestry centers, along with Lille, which continues its heritage today as a mostly industrial textile city. In addition, in the 1700s northwestern France developed several local traditions of faience, some of the fanciest in the country, with styles similar to English wares. The region is also full of gastronomic pleasures, from Camembert cheese to Calvados, and Cointreau.

Perhaps France's most isolated region, both geographically and culturally, Brittany (or Bretagne) projects westward into the Atlantic Ocean. This region claims some of the most unique craft traditions in France, including the elaborate costumes with towerlike starched-lace headdresses of the local people, who are called *bigoudens*, and maritime crafts such as prow sculpting and sailcloth making. Brittany is home to vestiges of a rich prehistoric culture and shares a Celtic heritage with its English and Welsh neighbors just across the English Channel. Today, about a quarter of the population, especially older folk in the more isolated inland hamlets, still speak *Breton*, a Celtic tongue that resembles Welsh.

Farther to the east, Normandy is famous as the home of William the Conqueror and as the site of the most crucial battles of World War II. These days Norman beaches are dotted with exclusive vacation towns, and the region boasts France's most important center of copper working, Villedieu-les-Poêles, as well as lace, tapestry, and faience making. The Nord-Pas-de-Calais region, just a short distance from England's southern shores, shares cultural and artisanal traditions with its Anglo-Saxon neighbors. The castle-filled Loire Valley hugs the region to the south, marking the gateway to the southwest.

THE TRADITIONS

COPPERWARE

Cuivre

Where else but France, a country in which culinary culture reigns supreme, would you expect to find such high-quality cookware? Since the dawn of time, cooks have prized copper for its malleability, durability, and excellent heat conduction. Copper is mined all over France, but the little town of Villedieu-les-Poêles (*poêles* means pots) claims copper as its raison d'être.

The history of copper in Villedieu-les-Poêles stretches back to the eleventh century, when the Hospitallers, a militaristic order of monks, founded the town and began mining and working copper. By the eighteenth century, more than a hundred copper artisans were turning out domestic wares, and Villedieu became known throughout France as a *cité du cuivre*.

Copper is infinitely malleable when heated to high temperatures. Originally, coppersmiths pressed the metal into sheets and then hammered them into bowl or pot shapes, leaving a characteristic mottled appearance. Alternatively, they heated the material to a molten state and poured it into molds for a smoother effect. Today, many copper pots are lined with stainless steel, which makes them easier to cook with, not to mention clean. Professional-quality vessels are sometimes lined with tin, which heats evenly but needs to be redone occasionally. Handles in bronze, stainless steel, or iron are often riveted onto the vessel. Generally, the thicker the pot, the higher the quality. Pots of two and a half to three millimeters are considered good quality.

Today, much of the copperware production in Villedieu-les-Poêles is fabricated industrially, in factories scattered on the outskirts of town. A few artisanal producers maintain a more handmade approach in smaller ateliers in town. In other cases, production is a compromise between machine-pressed sheets and hand-finishing.

The high cost of labor in France has driven many artisan coppersmiths out of business in recent decades, and their wares have been replaced by cheaper imports. Unfortunately, some shops in France—even in Villedieu-les-Poêles—carry a mix of locally made and imported wares, and at first glance it is not easy to tell the difference. If you want a handmade pot, be sure to buy directly from the artisan whenever possible, and look for pieces stamped with a hallmark, usually on the bottom of the pot or under the handle, as described below.

L'ORIGINAL

Most locally made wares are stamped with a "Villedieu" hallmark, sometimes in combination with a Maltese cross, the sign of the Knights of Saint John, who were descended from the Hospitallers that founded Villedieu-les-Poêles.

ÇA COUTE COMBIEN?

Expect to pay around 300 to 500 euros for a quality set of pots, but also consider shipping costs. These wares are hefty; you may pay 100 euros or more to get them home.

CRÈME DE LA CRÈME

L'Atelier du Cuivre (page 98) provides a good opportunity to see copper makers in action.

TEXTILE ARTS: LACE AND COSTUMES

Dentelle et Costume

T apestry and lace making were two of northwestern France's primary industries up through the French Revolution, and distinctive local traditions thrived in Brittany and Normandy. Bayeux and Alençon in Normandy were renowned throughout the country for their distinctive lace patterns, and smaller towns (including the copper capital of Villedieu-les-Poêles) boasted their own prolific communities of lace makers. Though primarily the province of women, men sometimes participated in this craft as well.

What's fascinating about the history of lace is that the styles were as individualized as the towns themselves. Bayeux was known for its sometimes-black bobbin lace, Alençon for its refined white needle lace. Each tradition carries a different story. *Point d'Alençon*, perhaps the most famous Norman lace, was so esteemed that it was even called *point de France*. According to legend, around 1650 Marthe La Perrière, the widow of a local surgeon in Alençon, took it upon herself to imitate *point de Venise*, the Venetian needle lace that was all the rage in Europe at the time. She altered the basic design to form what later became known as *point d'Alençon*, farming

out different parts of the process to local women to speed production and market-ing the final product herself. Jean-Baptiste Colbert, Louis XIV's finance minister, founded a new royal lace *manufacture* in Alençon in 1665, forming a monopoly that eventually became so prolific that it employed some seven thousand people on the eve of the French Revolution. The Alençon *manufacture* catered to consumers hun-gry for this high-status lace to embellish their clothes and decorate their homes.

Another unique lace story comes from Brittany. Between 1902 and 1907, sardines—the basis of the region's most profitable industry—disappeared from the coastal waters, and as a result many families faced financial ruin and starvation. Breton crochet lace, known as *picot bigouden*, became an unlikely savior. Knowing that production of a similar kind of fashionable crochet lace had saved many families from poverty during the infamous Potato Famine that ravaged Ireland in the mid-nineteenth century, several charitable French aristocrats and nuns began teaching the craft to *bigouden* women and children (both girls and boys). Used to working on nets, fishermen's wives and children started churning out crochet lace with cotton threads, both for clothing and household use, and even selling their work door to door; people marveled at the women with curious Breton costumes and headdresses hawking their wares on the streets of France and throughout Europe. The openwork patterns often incorporated Celtic motifs dear to the Breton people. The lace was a hit in Parisian boutiques, and flourished until after World War I, when fashions changed and cheaper machine-made lace became more common.

Breton artisans still create a more elaborate type of lace, which you can appre-ciate in the intricate *coiffes*, or traditional tall headdresses of the *bigoudines*. Many of these starched-lace *coiffes* are further embellished with embroidery, representing hours of additional labor. The *coiffe* tops off an often equally elaborate dress, skirt, and apron, also featuring embroidery and sometimes lace. Typically worn today only during important festivals and folkloric events, a handful of mostly elderly women continue to don these fantastic outfits every day.

L'ORIGINAL

Today it is possible to find little treasures of antique Breton crochet lace in antiques shops and markets around Finistère, and a few elderly inhabitants continue to wear and sell it.

ÇA COUTE COMBIEN?

Considering that a square centimeter of *point d'Alençon* takes some fifteen hours of labor, it's no wonder that a little piece can cost hundreds of euros.

CRÈME DE LA CRÈME
The lace cooperative in Bayeux, Conservatoire de la Dentelle (page 97) provides a rare opportunity to observe this painstaking craft up close.

FAIENCE

Faïence

s in the case of lace, it seems that every corner of northwestern France boasts its own local tradition of faience, or glazed ceramics with colorful patterns on a white background. Historically, the region's most important centers of faience production were Desvres, in the Nord-Pas-de-Calais area; Rouen, in Normandy; Malicorne-sur-Sarthe, in the Loire Valley; and finally, Rennes and Quimper, in Brittany. Of these, only HB-Henriot of Quimper flourishes today as a company of international repute, thanks in large part to its smart marketing campaign to portray its wares as synonymous with French country style. In other towns, which once boasted huge cottage industries, just a few torchbearers now carry on their faience traditions.

FAIENCE VERSUS POTTERY: WHEN A POT IS NOT JUST A POT

The French consider *poterie* and *faïence* two completely different things, a distinction that causes confusion among many casual travelers, for whom a pot is just a pot. Here's the difference:

Poterie

Pottery means simply humble, utilitarian wares—pitchers, plates, bowls, cups, or urns—for the table or garden. Craftspeople have made these wares for centuries to meet their basic needs. A lot of northern French pottery is stoneware, made from a particular type of hard earth that can withstand high firing temperatures, and it is suitable for cooking. Pottery may or may not have decoration, and may be fired in a kiln once or twice. A *potier* makes *poterie*.

Faience

Faience is fancier and more complicated to produce. The word *faïence* is a Frenchified version of the name Faenza, the town in central Italy known for its production of these colorful wares (the Italian term *maiolica*, which describes the Italian wares, is more or less synonymous with faience). The hallmark of faience is colorful decoration against a shiny white background, achieved with a bath in enamel or tin-based glazes, and two firings. Faience usually means earthenware, made from ruddy clay that can be fired only at relatively low temperatures, and it may not be used for cooking. Therefore, most faience is purely decorative.

The golden age of French faience was the seventeenth and eighteenth centuries, when Asian imports set the style and colorful, translucent wares were sought after by the courts and the bourgeoisie. Rouen, Nevers, Quimper, and Moustiers-Sainte-Marie figured among France's top faience centers. Someone who makes faience is a *faïencier*.

In France, ceramics traditions run deep and wide. Each region boasts a complex history of ceramics, and the number of terms used to describe these wares is mind-boggling. So far we haven't even mentioned the type of ceramic wares called porcelain—*excusez-moi, porcelaine*. For that, see the section on Limoges (chapter 4).

Faience flourished in France in the seventeenth and eighteenth centuries, when imported Asian porcelain became en vogue among the aristocracy. French artisans were inspired to interpret in their own style the glossy, milky white wares decorated with bright colors. The Chinese decorative vocabulary was superseded by a purely French one, and pieces were adorned with flowers, flourishes, and figural decoration known today as chinoiserie for its reliance on Asian models. Most of the *faïenciers* working in these regions in the eighteenth century were well aware of the faience being produced in other centers of southern and eastern France—including Nevers and Moustiers-Sainte-Marie. Artisans moved freely from town to town, and *faïenciers* even married into faience families in other towns, making for an often fascinating mélange of styles.

Although today it ranks a distant second to Quimper in terms of commercial success, Rouen was the region's most important center of production in the eighteenth-century heyday. Its designs were celebrated for their similarity to Chinese models, and these ornate wares decorated châteaux and state buildings across France. Unfortunately, only a few *faïenciers* are still active in Rouen.

All of these centers followed the same basic techniques for creating faience: firing clay to a biscuit, covering it with a white opaque glaze, applying painted decoration, and then firing it again to achieve the final piece. Many of the northern French faience patterns are fancy and feminine. The wares of Desvres resemble the equally fussy styles of English ceramics—not surprisingly given the town's proximity to the English Channel. Artisans in Rouen and Rennes also produced delicate, ornate wares with scalloped edges and floral designs.

Today, a single enterprise perpetuates the tradition of Quimper faience—HB-Henriot. In 1690, Jean-Baptiste Bousquet, a potter from Provence who had learned his trade in Moustiers-Sainte-Marie, headed north to Brittany and founded a faience shop. His granddaughter married a *faïencier* from Nevers, and their daughter married a *faïencier* from Rouen. Encapsulating most of the faience traditions of France in this one family, their invention was to incorporate the color red into the repertoire of decorations. After the French Revolution, Antoine de la Hubaudière took over, and in the nineteenth century the company's folkloristic style became synonymous with Quimper. By the middle of the century, when the railroad linked Brittany to Paris, the company named itself HB (La Hubaudière-Bousquet), and found itself well on its way to a commercial success that would continue through the first half of the twentieth century. Jules Henriot, a rival in town, also produced popular pieces. The Henriot and HB families joined forces, and in 1968 the company began going by HB-Henriot. It now distributes its wares across

France and abroad in catalogues and stores—and at its factory in Quimper, where all the goods are still handmade.

L'ORIGINAL

Rouen is a bustling antiques town; at its markets you can sometimes ferret out a quality piece of faience dating back one hundred to two hundred years.

ÇA COUTE COMBIEN?

Faience is relatively affordable, but remember that you will need to carry on your purchase when flying home, or arrange for shipping for these fragile wares.

CRÈME DE LA CRÈME

HB-Henriot (page 95) is one of the region's most popular faience makers today.

THE LISTINGS

BRITTANY
(Bretagne)

Côtes d'Armor

DINAN

The medieval streets of Dinan, a popular destination for exploring, unfortunately are filled with many tourist traps, but you still come across good finds.

LACE AND EMBROIDERY

Fleur de Lin et Bouton d'Or
9 rue du Petit Fort
02 96 85 05 87
www.fleurdelinetboutondor.com

This antiques shop assembles a fascinating jumble of vintage Breton lace alongside antique ribbons, trims, and buttons that sell for just a few euros. Here you might discover a classic piece of *picot bigoudin*, a type of lace that local fishermen's wives began making after the sardine fishing crisis of the early 1900s, when they turned from making fishing nets to making doilies and other table adornments.

Finistère

LOCRONAN

Between the fourteenth and seventeenth centuries, the stone village of Locronan, near the western extremes of Brittany, was famous for its sailcloth. Though the industry eventually declined, Locronan still houses a lively community of weavers who specialize mostly in table linens.

LINENS

La Maison des Artisans Tissage du Lain
Place de l'Eglise
02 98 91 83 96

This shop sells locally made tablecloths as well as a wide variety of more mass-produced dish-cloths and napkins in traditional Breton designs. The most unusual offerings are bath towels, dishcloths, and bathrobes made of cloth woven from bamboo. Prices range between 15 and 200 euros.

Musée d'Art et d'Histoire
Town center
02 98 51 80 80

If you want to learn more about Locronan's history of sailcloth making, the museum is an excellent place to view several historical looms and see exhibitions about the town's weaving history. Alas, no shop.

PONT L'ABBÉ

Pont l'Abbé is one of the great bastions of *bigouden* culture. On Sundays and market days, you might glimpse ladies of a certain age wearing the stunning *coiffe bigoudène*, a towering lace head-dress that can reach a foot or more in height.

TRADITIONAL COSTUMES

Musée Bigouden
Mairie
Town center, Château Pont-L'Abbé
02 98 66 09 03

I guarantee that your jaw will drop when you see this collection's array of folkloric costumes from centuries past, replete with lace details and elaborate headdresses.

QUIMPER

Quimper is a fun destination, especially for lovers of French country style. If you like HB-Henriot's ceramic wares, you'll be in heaven.

FAIENCE

*Faïenceries HB-Henriot
Rue Haute
02 98 90 09 36
www.hb-henriot.com

Be sure to tour HB-Henriot's atelier, where you can observe several dozen workers quietly turning out the happy wares that have made this *faïencier* famous. Two rustic rooms welcome visitors on the ground floor of the shop, where you can view tableware and sculpture

from the current collection. Upstairs, you can pick up factory seconds at remarkably good prices: ceramic jewelry from 30 euros, plates for 50 to 70 euros, sculptures starting at 70 euros, and miniature Breton clogs that go for 10 euros and make easily transportable souvenirs. The store ships.

Musée de la Faience Jules Verlingue
14 rue Jean Baptiste Bousquet
02 98 90 12 72
www.musee-faience-quimper.com

The faience museum holds a collection of impressive wares from the eighteenth and nineteenth centuries, as well as rotating temporary exhibitions.

PAYS DE LA LOIRE

Maine-et-Loire

ANGERS

COINTREAU

Musée Cointreau
Zone Industrielle Saint-Barthélemy
   Carrefour
Saint-Barthélemy d'Anjou
02 41 31 50 50
www.cointreau.com

Brothers Adolphe and Edouard-Jean Cointreau founded this artisanal distillery in Angers in 1849; their unique innovation was the inclusion of orange peels into this distinctive French *digestif*. Its current owners, the wine and spirits group Rémy-Cointreau, which also owns the Rémy Martin brand (chapter 5), runs a sleek visitor's center on the outskirts of the town, where you can learn about the production of Cointreau.

Sarthe

MALICORNE-
SUR-SARTHE

Although people have been working clay in the Sarthe Valley since ancient times, artisans in the village of Malicorne-sur-Sarthe began their tradition of brightly colored, enameled faience only in the eighteenth century; according to legend, they were influenced by a traveling faïencier from Nevers. Eventually,

Malicorne's own faïenciers became known for openwork edges (these pieces are referred to as *ajouré*) and a highly refined decorative style with rich blues and ochre tones.

FAIENCE

Faïenceries d'art du bourg Joly
16 rue Carnot
02 43 94 80 10

In addition to old-style faience, Joly's specialty is ceramic figures—saints and whimsical folkloric people in traditional dress, as well as animals such as country chickens.

Faïenceries d'art de Malicorne
18 rue Bernard-Palissy
02 43 94 81 18
www.faiencerie-malicorne.com

Victor and Stéphane Deschang operate their family *faïencerie* in the purest spirit of the historical traditions of Malicorne-sur-Sarthe. They and their assistants rely on a personal collection of local antique faience as the basis for their rich creations. My favorites are the plates and platters with openwork edges and refined designs. The quality and prices are high; you can expect to pay between 50 and 100 euros for a single plate.

LOWER NORMANDY
(Basse-Normandie)

Calvados

BAYEUX

Bayeux has been a textile center for many centuries. The impressive Bayeux Tapestry attests to a community of accomplished embroiderers dating back to the eleventh century. Later, lace making overtook tapestry as Bayeux's primary industry. By the eighteenth century, the town boasted more than fifteen hundred lace makers, and lace making had become the town's main industry. The industrial revolution sounded the death knell for textiles in the 1870s when machine-made lace eclipsed the handmade version, but it is worth a trek to Bayeux to appreciate its two historical crafts.

LACE AND EMBROIDERY

*Bayeux Tapestry
Centre Guillaume le Conquérant
13 Rue de Nesmond
02 31 51 25 50

Technically, this is not a tapestry at all but embroidery. Either way, it's one of the most incredible works in French art history. The seventy-meter-long Bayeux Tapestry recounts the history of William the Conqueror's deeds in England in the fateful year of 1066. This masterpiece of textile art lends some insight into the consummate skill of local embroiderers of centuries past.

Conservatoire de la Dentelle
Maison Adam & Eve
6 rue du Bienvenu
02 31 92 73 80
www.dentelledebayeux.free.fr

Once a thriving lace-making capital, Bayeux holds on to its lace-making status by a thread. In 1982, town officials opened the lace conservatory to preserve the history of this important craft, and to support the work of Mylène Salvador and Sylvie Mallard, as well as several other lace makers whose painstaking labor you can observe at this museum. Pick up a finely wrought souvenir in the boutique, or join a workshop if you want to learn to make lace yourself.

Manche

VILLEDIEU-LES-POÊLES

Thousands of shiny copper vessels hang from the ceilings and walls of the shops lining the main drag through Villedieu-les-Poêles. Most of the more industrial factories on the edge of town are closed to visitors, including Mauviel, which crafts professional-quality wares that are distributed through Williams-Sonoma stores and catalogues in the United States, and are favorites of chefs. Among the shops, it's not easy to discern who carries locally made wares, who offers cheaper imports, and who sells both—a particularly confusing scenario. To make sure you're getting a pot made by hand in Villedieu-les-Poêles, look for hallmarks stamped on the piece, ask a lot of questions, and whenever possible, buy directly from the artisan.

BELLS

Fonderie de Cloches
10 rue Pont Chignon
02 33 61 00 56
www.cornille-havard.com

Large-scale sculptures and bells are casually scattered on the grass in front of this foundry, which carries on a bell-making tradition started by Villedieu's medieval metalsmiths. Tour the fascinating atelier, where a guide will lead you through each step of production, from the crafting of wooden profiles to molding and casting huge bells using the lost-wax process. A small shop sells inexpensive souvenir bells and locally made copper pots.

COPPER

L'Atelier du Cuivre
54 rue du Général Huard
02 33 51 31 85

Duck behind the simple shop filled with stacks of just-finished pots and pans and take a tour of a working copperware atelier, where artisans are busily hammering and reheating molten copper. The shop sells small trinkets and pots and pans for 50 to 300 euros.

PEWTER

Guy Segoin
13 rue Carnot
02 33 61 08 54

The friendly Monsieur Segoin, a former mechanic, turned to pewter making and began re-creating traditional milking buckets, lamps, and other curiosities from Norman and Breton farm life. His World War II soldiers lined up in the window are particularly popular with visiting veterans.

Maison de l'Etain
15 rue du Général Huard
02 33 51 05 08

Run by the same folks who own the nearby L'Atelier du Cuivre, the atelier of Maison de l'Etain shows the process of crafting objects from pewter. The extensive shop sells affordably priced dishes, cups, and larger sculptures, starting at 10 euros.

Orne

ALENÇON

In the seventeenth and eighteenth centuries, *point d'Alençon*, an intricate type of lace made with a single needle and thread, was renowned in Europe as one of the most fashionable and luxurious types of adornment.

LACE

Atelier National du Point d'Alençon
13 rue Jullien
02 33 26 33 60

This excellent lace atelier run by the French ministry of culture perpetuates the otherwise-dead craft of *point d'Alençon*. A dozen or so artisans now work this detailed needle lace, some filling commissions for the state.

Musée des Beaux Arts et de la Dentelle
Cour Carrée de la Dentelle
12 rue Capit Charles Aveline
02 33 32 40 07

This museum displays breathtaking pieces of Alençon lace from the seventeenth to the twentieth centuries, and you can purchase small reproductions in its store.

UPPER NORMANDY
(Haute-Normandie)

Seine-Maritime

ROUEN

A beautiful Norman town, in terms of faience, Rouen is a mere shadow of its former glory: in the seventeenth and eighteenth centuries, it was the northwest's premier center for fancy ceramic wares. Start with the museum, then check out its two good artisanal producers for a taste of Rouen's ceramic heritage.

FAIENCE

Faïencerie Augy-Carpentier
26 rue Saint-Romain
02 35 88 77 47

Several women make faience in the atelier behind the shop—if you ask, you can take a look. You can also watch an artist hand-painting designs on plates and cups at a worktable in the front of the shop. For 30 euros and up, you can commission a cup or even an entire service with your name or family crest.

Faïence Saint Romain
56 rue Saint-Romain
02 35 07 12 30
www.faiences-rouen.com

Monsieur and Madame Petit are hard at work firing traditional dishware in the kiln inside this tiny store tucked away on a quiet street behind the cathedral. They share the space with a young painter who works near the window, adding finishing touches to the objects.

Musée de la Céramique
Hôtel d'Hocqueville
1 rue Faucon
02 35 07 31 74

Housed in an elegant seventeenth-century noble residence, this impressive display of some six thousand pieces of ceramics centers around the collection of André Pottier, a local expert of nineteenth-century faience from Rouen and elsewhere. Temporary exhibitions of contemporary ceramics round out the experience, but there is no shop.

NORD-PAS-DE-CALAIS

Pas de Calais

DESVRES

Locals have made pottery in Desvres since before Roman times, thanks to the ready availability of clay, water, and wood. However, it wasn't until 1804 that the town became synonymous with faience. François Fourmaintraux was inspired by delicate faience from England as well as other French centers, including Nevers, Rouen, and Moustiers-Sainte-Marie. Fourmaintraux's workshop propelled Desvres to a position as the most important faience-making center in the north of France, eclipsing Rouen's prominence, a distinction it held for nearly a century. Today, decorative wall tiles are some of the town's most typical products.

FAIENCE

Maison de la Faïence
Musée de la Céramique
Rue Jean Macé
03 21 83 23 23
www.desvresmuseum.org

This museum provides a good opportunity to view Desvres faience from its nineteenth-century heyday. The museum is also an active atelier, hosting several *faïenciers*-in-residence who take turns in this architecturally unique building with a roofline made to look like huge, slanting ceramic tiles.

Faïencerie d'Art Fourmaintraux
114 rue Jean Jaurès
03 21 91 65 55

This factory-like enterprise is the heir to the Fourmaintraux faience dynasty that catapulted Desvres to fame as a center of faience in the 1800s. You can visit and view all the stages of production, from molding to the final decoration and firing in large kilns.

PICARDY
(Picardie)

Oise

BEAUVAIS

Many of Beauvais's buildings were destroyed in World War II, including those housing the national tapestry works. During that time, many of its *tapissiers* had to transfer temporarily to Aubusson (chapter 4) and Gobelins (chapter 1). Thankfully, today the Beauvais tapestry tradition is again thriving.

TAPESTRIES

Galerie Nationale de la Tapisserie
22 rue Saint-Pierre
03 44 15 39 10

A museumlike showcase of Beauvais tapestry history, the Galerie Nationale de la Tapisserie hosts rotating exhibitions based on the *manufacture*'s archives and rich collections of tapestries and related objects from the Middle Ages to the present. The old tapestry patterns, or *cartons*, some painted by the most esteemed artists of the day, are especially interesting.

Manufacture Nationale de la Tapisserie
24 rue Henri Brispot
03 44 14 41 90

To compete with the famed Flemish textiles, this tapestry works was deemed a royal *manufacture* by French minister Jean-Baptiste Colbert during his sweeping royal arts campaign under Louis XIV. You can still find a legion of weavers here—called *tapissiers* or *lissiers*—working on traditional and contemporary designs. The Beauvais technique, or *basse lisse*, means that the tapestry maker works on a horizontal surface, as opposed to *haute lisse*, in which the work is done on a vertical surface, as in Aubusson (chapter 4). The Beauvais tapestry factory remains a national cultural institution, producing tapestries for state buildings and diplomatic gifts.

Somme

AMIENS

MARIONETTES

*Pierre Facquier
67 rue du Don
03 22 92 49 52

The historical province of Picardy once possessed a lively tradition of marionettes; nearly every town drew crowds to the local marionette theaters, where beloved characters performed comedic productions in the local Picard language. Similar to the popular Guignol character of the Lyonnais marionette theaters (chapter 4), the hero of Picard theater was Lafleur, a mischievous everyman who got himself into droll situations, to the delight of audiences. Through the early twentieth century, there were some two dozen theaters in Amiens performing these three-hundred-year-old "sitcoms." Today, Pierre Facquier is the sole torchbearer of this tradition. In his workshop near the glorious cathedral of Amiens, Facquier uses walnut, cherry, and apple woods to craft the bodies of the characters; his wife, Madame Facquier, makes their historically accurate clothes. You can watch a show at their theater and purchase a marionette for 100 to 300 euros.

BELGIUM

LUXEMBOURG

GERMANY

Chartres •

• Tours   Gien •
• Villaines-les-Rochers   Saint-Amand-en-Puisaye

CENTRE   La Borne •   BURGUNDY
                                    (Bourgogne)   Dijon •

• Bourges   • Nevers   FRANCHE-COMTÉ

Limoges •   Aubusson   Moirans-en-Montagne   SWITZERLAND
        •   •   Saint-Claude •

LIMOUSIN   AUVERGNE   Chamonix-
                  Ambert •   • Lyon   Mont Blanc
                                                    •
Thiers •   Brioude •   RHÔNE-ALPES
                                    • Saint-Jean-de-Maurienne
        Le Puy •   • Grenoble

                                    ITALY

Chapter 4:

CENTRAL AND EASTERN FRANCE

❧

The country's breadbasket, France's central and eastern regions are near and dear to my heart. I spent a formative college year in Lyon and believe that the city is one of the country's best-kept secrets, holding fantastic artistic and culinary surprises. Research projects took me to the Auvergne, where I fell in love with France's most rural region, with its craft traditions, architectural styles, and agricultural communities that perpetuate centuries-old ways of life.

Each of the regions that makes up this enormous chunk of France—Auvergne, Burgundy, Centre, Franche-Comté, Limousin, and Rhône-Alpes—is culturally distinct and artisanally rich in its own right. Historically, this part of France has been subject to numerous influences and counts several town-specific traditions that are world famous: Limoges porcelain, Le Puy bobbin lace, Auvergnat knives, Dijon mustard, Millau gloves, and Lyonnais silk, to name a few.

Within this large geographical area, Burgundy stands apart both historically and culturally. Through the fifteenth century, when the duchy was finally annexed to France, the dukes of Burgundy wielded great economic and political power. This aristocratic heritage is the basis for many of its local craft traditions, from faience to heavy, ornate furniture, and a distinctive regional architecture that reflects the tastes of its wealthy patrons. Add to this specific gastronomic delights such as its wine and mustard, and special liqueurs made with grapes, including cassis.

From handmade lace to knives, puppets, and of course, various culinary and oenological traditions, it could take a lifetime to get to know all the grand traditions and folkloric delights of the heart of France.

THE TRADITIONS

AUBUSSON TAPESTRY

Tapisserie d'Aubusson

 ubusson, east of the porcelain capital of Limoges, is known for the luxurious tradition of tapestry. At one time, these labor-intensive textiles decorated the cold stone walls of châteaux and noble homes across France, providing practical insulation as well as sumptuous adornment.

Like so many French craft traditions, the availability of unique local natural and human resources nurtured the development of tapestry production in Aubusson. The crystal-clear, rushing waters of the Creuse River provided the perfect medium for creating the richly hued dyes used to color the woolen threads. A community of skilled weavers assembled in Aubusson, and the mythological, historical, and religious images they created were celebrated in noble homes across France.

The glory days of Aubusson were the sixteenth through the eighteenth centuries. The town reached its height of production after Jean-Baptiste Colbert, one of Louis XIV's chief ministers and an avid patron of the arts (himself the son of a draper), established Aubusson as a royal tapestry *manufacture*. Over the course of the seventeenth and eighteenth centuries, the Aubusson *manufacture* supplied the French court with tapestries as well as draperies and upholstery; these tapestries spread across Europe as well. Today, no important château or state building in France is without one.

The rushing waters of the Creuse, which runs through the center of Aubusson, were corralled for the process of *teinture*, or dyeing yarn. It's the quality of dyeing as well as the density of the weave that determines how long a tapestry will last, and durability became one of the hallmarks of Aubusson tapestry. A single tapestry begins with a maquette, or preparatory sketch, which may be a drawing, pastel, oil sketch, or fully elaborated oil painting. Some of the most famous artists from the past three centuries have created maquettes, often oil paintings, to be reproduced as Aubusson tapestries. The maquette is then translated into a *carton*, or a kind of "weave by numbers pattern," which the artisans use to produce the woven version. In Aubusson, weavers used the *haute lisse* technique, meaning that they worked a vertical loom (as opposed to *basse lisse*, the horizontal loom method used in Beauvais).

In the late eighteenth century, the French Revolution suppressed the monarchy and patterned wallpaper became all the rage; as a result, the tapestry industry began to decline. Unlike Beauvais and Gobelins, Aubusson is no longer a state *manufacture* today, yet even through the nineteenth century the local economy supported thousands of *tapissiers.* The industrial revolution later transformed Aubusson into a center of carpet and rug production, one of the most important in France. Some rug manufacturers work on special order only and continue to produce items for important French government buildings and private clients.

Thanks to the efforts of a local artist, Jean Lurçat, the 1930s and 1940s saw the re-emergence of artisanal tapestry in Aubusson, and weavers unearthed the old designs to serve as inspirations for new creations. Fortunately, today a small community of faithful weavers continues the tradition of handmade tapestries that originally put this Limousin town on the map.

L'ORIGINAL

A custom-made rug—for the floor or wall—is a special treat that can bring a uniquely French accent to your interior, and the accomplished *tapissiers* in Aubusson can whip up a design of your dreams.

ÇA COUTE COMBIEN?

A quality Aubusson tapestry may set you back several thousand euros, but with proper care will last a lifetime.

CRÈME DE LA CRÈME

Robert Four (page 125) is the king of historically accurate tapestries from Aubusson's heyday, utilizing actual maquettes from the eighteenth century to create modern-day masterpieces.

BASKETRY

Vannerie

asket making was one of France's largest industries through the nineteenth century, employing tens of thousands of craftspeople hard at work weaving straw, reeds, and grasses by hand. These rustic containers were used to hold the harvest, personal goods, and most importantly, bread. The invention of the cardboard box, along with other types of containers ushered in by the industrial revolution, spelled the demise of the French *panier*, or bread basket. Today just two villages carry on this centuries-old tradition: Fayl-Billot in Champagne and the hamlet of Villaines-les-Rochers in the Centre region, which boasts an impressive production of wicker baskets.

Basket making is recorded as far back as the sixteenth century in Villaines-les-Rochers. Craftspeople mostly churned out utilitarian baskets for the villagers, but eventually, in the mid-twentieth century, they began making larger-scale objects, including furniture. This labor-intensive craft begins with willow reeds, or *osier*, which grow in abundance in and around this picturesque village. During the winter, the long, rodlike twigs are harvested, sorted into neat piles, and bundled according to size for weaving.

Geography plays a key role in the endurance of the basketry tradition in Villaines-les-Rochers. First, the town is located in a valley, the humidity of which is perfect for cultivating various species of willow. Second, it includes some one thousand underground caves that provide stable levels of humidity, which keeps the reeds stored there supple—some basket weavers even operate their ateliers inside these troglodytic studios.

Today, some seventy basket weavers work year-round making *paniers*, serving trays, platters, and garden ornaments, as well as more unusual furnishings and decorative objects. A cooperative with more than a century of history oversees the production and helps merchandise its members' products, especially in the busy wholesale market that supplies countless *boulangeries* and *pâtisseries*—bread and pastry shops—which use baskets as the central furnishings of their establishments. As with so many French crafts, basket making evolved in the service of food, and today, many of the *paniers* made in Villaines-les-Rochers end up in bread shops around the country, where they hold the day's bread, hot from the oven—a true French tradition, indeed. Amazingly, the weavers in this humble town churn out more than half of France's basket production.

L'ORIGINAL
Paniers, or bread baskets like the ones you find in the *boulangeries*, are one of the best French souvenirs you can buy, and a handmade one from Villaines-les-Rochers is a great choice.

ÇA COUTE COMBIEN?
You may be surprised at the relatively high prices of baskets in Villaines-les-Rochers, which reflect the high cost of labor in France as well as the painstaking nature of this craft. Expect to spend around 100 euros for a simple basket, several hundred for a classic French *boulangerie* model, and even more for a custom piece such as a bassinet or garden ornament.

CRÈME DE LA CRÈME
Vannerie de Villaines (page 123), home of the town's basket cooperative, assembles the work of its best weavers.

DIJON MUSTARD

Moutarde de Dijon

The secret of authentic Dijon mustard lies in the fermentation process of the mustard seed, an alchemical reaction that Burgundian mustard makers, or *moutardiers,* understood as far back as the Middle Ages. Part of the success of Dijon mustard has to do with the town's location along one of the major spice routes to the Far East, which transported the flavors of many cultures to and from Europe. For centuries, gourmands have prized this pungent condiment; they purchased it from *moutardiers,* who sold their goods door to door and advised how to use it with meats, vegetables, eggs, and bread.

You may wonder what all the fuss is about—until you taste it. In its raw state, the miniscule *brassica nigra* mustard seed contains little spiciness. Once fermented, however, it develops the sharp tang that is now associated with Dijon mustard. Originally fermented in vinegar, by the eighteenth century producers began steeping the seed in the juice of unripened local grapes (*verjus*), and therein lies the key to authentic Dijonnais flavor. After being soaked in the *verjus*, the mustard seeds are finely ground and strained, then mixed with the other ingredients, including vinegar, sugar, and spices, to make the final product.

Dijon mustard is regulated like wine and enjoys it own appellation. This rigorous process of certification ensures a consistently smooth, golden, and pungent-tasting final product. The official designation is seed-specific and not geographical; therefore, authentic Dijon mustard may be made anywhere in France as long as it follows the traditional preparation. However, the most famous and historic makers still call Dijon home, and the city remains synonymous with its famous *moutarde.*

The craft of mustard making spawned a second artisanal tradition—the pots that contain this precious condiment. Potters across Burgundy churned out little mustard pots marked with trademarks, logos, or just the word *moutarde,* sometimes accompanied by a special spoon. These squat crocks, sometimes sealed with wax or another airtight lid, have been produced for centuries. In the old days, townspeople brought their empty *pots à moutarde* to be refilled from the giant vats at the local mustard shop. Though potters continue to make these little treasures today, antique mustard pots are prized collectibles.

L'ORIGINAL
Although you can buy Dijon mustard all over the world, in Dijon you'll encounter a stunning variety of local gourmet mustards you won't find elsewhere, from peppercorn to raspberry, walnut, and tarragon.

ÇA COUTE COMBIEN?
At just a few euros, Dijon mustard makes an excellent value for one of France's great traditions.

CRÈME DE LA CRÈME
Maille, founded in 1742, is the oldest producer of Dijon mustard, and a pot of it from its flagship store in Dijon is a classic Burgundian souvenir (page 120). The well-known Grey Poupon company was founded in Dijon some thirty years later; it's now owned by Kraft Foods.

FAIENCE AND POTTERY

Faïence et poterie

Burgundy boasts two ceramics hubs: Nevers for faience, and Saint-Amand-en-Puisaye for pottery. In the Centre region, Gien is the faience capital, and La Borne the pottery center. The rise in prominence of these towns has much to do with the availability of good local clay conducive for creating the works, not to mention the skill of those working it.

Of these four ceramics centers, surely the most well-known is Gien. Gien is not only the name of the town renowned for these wares, but also the brand name of the *faïencerie* that makes the colorful pieces. The Gien faience works was founded in 1821 by Thomas Hall, an Englishman who is credited with bringing fancy English styles of faience to France. The location was carefully chosen for its combination of good clay in the soil, plenty of trees for firing the kilns, and access to the nearby Loire River for transporting the finished wares. Today, the Faïencerie de Gien repeats many of its most popular designs with more delicate English styles and sensibilities. In the 1980s, the company began an aggressive export strategy to the United States and Japan. Using Baccarat to distribute its products in North America saved it from folding, and explains why Gien is better known than other French ceramic wares.

Less known today but more prominent historically, Nevers, in Burgundy, was a major center for faience. During the sixteenth century, when the Italian Gonzaga family ruled Nevers, some of Emilia-Romagna's best artisans brought the technique of tin-glazing, central to making faience, to the town. Local *faïenciers* began to replicate these vessels, with ornate styles and bright colors against a shiny white background. The golden age of Nevers faience was the seventeenth century, when artisans sought to replicate the styles of porcelain imported from Asia. Today, Nevers boasts a handful of good artisans who employ only handmade techniques.

The ornate faience of Gien and Nevers seems light-years away from the humble pottery of Saint-Amand-en-Puisaye in Burgundy. Saint-Amand has been a pottery center for many centuries; documents attest to potters working the kilns there in the Middle Ages, creating what is perhaps France's most purely utilitarian pottery. The locally available clay, a variety known as *grès* that is coveted for its durability, is perfect for creating long-lasting plates, bowls, pitchers, and other rustic tableware. What distinguishes the pottery of Saint-Amand-en-Puisaye is that the clay is mixed with sand, and the wares are fired at very high temperatures, usually

1,250 to 1,290 degrees Celsius. This technique imparts a shiny, durable, and particularly water-resistant finish that is prized all over France.

In the Centre region, the village of La Borne has also been a busy hub of rustic, utilitarian *poterie* since the late Middle Ages. In cavernous kilns throughout town, several dozen *potiers* churn out no-frills tableware, as well as human-shaped vessels and statues that have become a hallmark of La Borne. In addition to these human forms, historically the town's potters crafted other *objets vivants,* including animal-shaped whistles, or *sifflets,* that are coveted collectors' items. The town has become something of a Bohemian artists' colony, attracting artisans from around the globe to its annual pottery celebrations.

L'ORIGINAL

Gien makes faience of various quality, from run-of-the-mill tableware with stenciled designs to fully handmade art pieces. Prices are a general indication of the quality, and helpful salespeople at the factory outlet (page 124) and the Paris showrooms (pages 44 and 53) can show you what is what.

To be sure you are buying authentic Nevers faience, look for the hallmark—an arabesque knot painted on the back of a vessel.

ÇA COUTE COMBIEN?

Antique pieces of Gien faience are some of France's most coveted collectibles; desirable single plates may fetch hundreds of euros at Gien's annual December auction (see Calendar of Events).

CRÈME DE LA CRÈME

Espace Céramique Jacques-Jeanneney (page 121) in Saint-Amand-en-Puisaye is a good place to buy these rustic wares.

LIMOGES PORCELAIN

Porcelaine de Limoges

L imoges is synonymous with porcelain, one of France's most famous craft traditions. These beautiful wares, valued for their translucence and fine workmanship, are distributed and celebrated around the globe.

The milky white porcelain is possible thanks to kaolin, a white clay found in natural deposits around the world. In the eighteenth century, kaolin was discovered eighteen miles from Limoges in Saint-Yrieix-la-Perche. People recognized its potential, and in the 1770s, an established faience factory in Limoges turned to creating porcelain with it; later, this factory would become the Manufacture Royale de Limoges.

Porcelain results from a unique recipe that consists of 50 percent kaolin, 25 percent feldspar, and 25 percent quartz. It's this combination that creates the translucent, shiny finish coveted by collectors around the world. Most pieces are built in a mold and undergo a first firing before being painted. A second firing imparts the lustrous sheen that is associated with Limoges ware.

Though there are many producers of Limoges porcelain, four big names dominate the town, and still produce its best wares: Ancienne Manufacture Royale de Limoges, Bernardaud, Haviland, and Raynaud. All four boast an impressive artisanal history and continue to produce wares that are, at least in part, handmade.

Of these, Bernardaud is a powerhouse international brand, with millions of euros in annual revenue and boutiques on some of the world's most prestigious streets, from New York's Park Avenue to the rue Royale in Paris. Despite its reputation within the luxury-goods market, Bernardaud thankfully has resisted corporate facelessness and remains a family enterprise with a truly artisanal soul. This famous *manufacture* was established in 1863 on the residential outskirts of Limoges. Today, the hallmark of its pieces, beautifully wrapped in its signature turquoise box, is an insistence on tradition but with an updated, modern feel.

While each of the big-name houses has its own trademark style, one of the most universally coveted types of Limoges ware is the historical *bleu de four*, or royal blue pieces often enhanced with gilding. Limoges boxes are also popular collectors' items; these miniscule receptacles come in thousands of shapes, from cowboy hats to mini Eiffel Towers, hamburgers, and shopping bags, or the classic box with floral designs and gold trim. Special ones are created for the American and Japanese markets.

While Limoges eventually became famous for its porcelain, during the Middle Ages and the Renaissance the city was renowned for another craft—enamel. This lesser-known yet older tradition involves a complex technique of mixing glazes and powders to create saturated colors of enamel on metal for a cloisonné effect. The medieval examples in Limoges's museums are so breathtakingly beautiful that the versions that several companies produce today, though labor-intensive, are laughable attempts to recapture this once-radiant art. When it comes to buying, stick to the porcelain.

L'ORIGINAL
What's special about the big Limoges porcelain houses is that although they are world-recognized brands, all four are still family operations, and much of the production is still carried out by hand.

ÇA COUTE COMBIEN?
A typical Limoges pill box will set you back about 100 to 150 euros.

CRÈME DE LA CRÈME
The Bernardaud factory and store (page 126) is a fascinating foray into the world of Limoges porcelain, with the town's best porcelain tour. Call ahead in the off-season (October to April).

SILK

Soie

I n its golden age of the early eighteenth century, Lyon counted an astonishing fifteen thousand silk workers toiling away in the service of nobility and royalty across France. No French nobleperson worth his or her
salt was without a cloak, a set of drapes, or bed linens made in Lyon.

In the fifteenth century, Louis XI installed a royal drapery *manufacture* in Lyon,
but the city rocketed to fame as a silk capital in 1531 under François I, who granted
it a monopoly for supplying silk not only to the court but to the entire kingdom. A
group of Italian drapers—renowned across Europe for its skill—moved in, and Lyon
soon eclipsed Italy as a silk-making capital. By the era of Louis XVI in the eighteenth century, Lyon's silk industry was producing luxurious fabrics that were fashioned into some of the fanciest clothes and home decor items in history, including
Marie-Antoinette's deluxe personal suite at Versailles.

Silkworms were cultivated all over France during this time, especially around
Lyon. Mulberry trees, which provided the worms' home and food, even graced the
Tuileries Gardens in Paris. To produce raw silk in the factories, cocoons were harvested and briefly boiled, which helped to unwind the delicate threads. Next, these
threads were "thrown," a process in which the strands were wound together to yield
a thicker, stronger yarn. The yarns were reboiled and dyed, after which they were
ready to be worked. The Lyonnais silk workers were called *canuts*, and were organized into a kind of early labor union, clustered in the Croix Rousse section of
Lyon. The Lyonnais also invented a specific type of loom for silk weaving, the *métier
à bras*, as well as many other handmade, specialized wooden and metal tools—all
uniquely Lyonnais—for weaving and finishing silks.

The French Revolution, and with it the abrupt halt in demand for luxury goods,
ended Lyon's silk industry with a sudden and thunderous crash, sending many silk

houses and their employees into financial ruin. Though the industry resurged some-
what in the nineteenth century, changing economic conditions and two large-scale
canut revolts spelled the end of Lyon's heyday as one of Europe's most important silk
cities. Today, Lyonnais silks retain a certain status in interior design, and two heirs to
the grand tradition (see below) are considered among the most prestigious in France.

L'ORIGINAL

Guignol, the leading character in the Lyonnais marionette theater (page 128),
is a silk worker, or *canut*.

ÇA COUTE COMBIEN?

Because Lyonnais silks still claim stature in the world of interior design, they
command comparatively high prices.

CRÈME DE LA CRÈME

Lyon's grand silk tradition is held in the hands of just two enterprises: Prelle (page
129) and Tassinari & Chatel, which you can see at Lelièvre in Paris (page 39).

WOOD CRAFTS (TOYS AND PIPES)

Artisanat en bois (jouets et pipes)

The Franche-Comté region shares many cultural traditions with Switzerland, which borders it to the east. Among its customary crafts are clock
making and toy making, as well as hand-carved pipes.

One factor that unites these otherwise disparate métiers is that they can
be carried out indoors during this mountainous region's long winter months.

Another is that they involve the special skill of wood turning, a process which created a cylindrical form that could be decorated like a tin soldier or other figure. According to local lore, this tradition of wood turning began when artisans gathered branches from the forests to make toys and rosary beads, which were sold to the throngs of pilgrims who made their way through the mountains to the churches in the region. Toy makers have been documented in the little town of Moirans-en-Montagne as far back as the twelfth century, and it remains an important French toy-making hub, though alas, most of it is now industrialized.

Eventually, this expertise in wood turning extended to other crafts. Saint-Claude, in the Jura region of the Franche-Comté, for example, has been synonymous with pipe making since the mid-nineteenth century. Its beautiful and ornate handcrafted smoker's pipes are made with wood from the area known to be resistant to fire. This painstaking art of pipe making begins with the roots of briarwood trees, *bruyère*, which grow in the local forests. Pipe makers harvest only the part of the root that lies on top of the soil, preserving the tree. The tree must be at least fifty years old, which, according to the pipe makers, gives the tobacco a unique flavor. The roots are boiled and dried, then cut into a rough pipe shape. Later, the mouthpiece, usually of amber, acrylic, or ebonite, is attached. Although many once-artisanal pipe makers evolved into large-scale industrial enterprises, individual Jurassian pipe makers remain true sculptors, crafting their pipes in the form of people, animal heads, and other remarkable shapes.

L'ORIGINAL
Few of Saint-Claude's pipe makers still harvest the roots of the *bruyère* tree themselves. Many pipes today are made with briarwood roots from Morocco, Algeria, Corsica, and Italy.

ÇA COUTE COMBIEN?
Machine-made pipes go for around 20 euros; a handcrafted model runs in the hundreds.

CRÈME DE LA CRÈME
Butz-Choquin (page 125), one of Saint-Claude's most prolific and more industrialized pipe makers, also turns out some stunning handwrought models.

THE LISTINGS

AUVERGNE

Haute-Loire

BRIOUDE

LACE

Hôtel de la Dentelle
29 and 43 rue du Quatre Septembre
04 71 74 80 02
www.hoteldeladentelle.com

This establishment, founded by local artisan Odette Arpin, is the only one to carry on the distinct tradition of multicolored lace known as *Cluny de Brioude*. Similar to the lace of Le Puy (see following entry), *Cluny de Brioude* is fashioned using many bobbins, but the threads are more colorful. The resulting pieces are often destined for the haute-couture industry. Contact the Hôtel de la Dentelle to ask about courses in lace making.

LE PUY

One of the oldest centers of lace making in France and one of the country's most unusual townscapes, Le-Puy-en-Velay is also one of my favorite places. Trudging up hundreds of stairs to its cavernous medieval cathedral, you pass aged women sitting in the shadows of their doorways, working bobbin lace just as their mothers and grandmothers did. What's unique about this meticulous métier in Le Puy is the use of a square piece of straw (*le carreau*) mounted between wooden supports that provides the workspace for these intricate lace patterns. The lace maker pins the pattern onto the straw background, and works it by moving the bobbins around. According to legend, the *carreau* method was born in 1407 when the bishop of Le Puy charged local lace maker Isabelle Mamour with the task of creating a sumptuous new outfit for the cathedral's

statue of the Black Virgin, venerated each year by thousands of pilgrims. According to the story, the *carreau* method allowed Mamour to finish the garment in record time, and other lace makers in town followed suit.

LACE

Atelier Conservatoire National de la Dentelle à la Main
38 and 42 rue Raphaël
04 71 02 01 68

The industrial revolution, which brought machine-made lace to Le Puy and elsewhere, nearly obliterated the town's important lace-making tradition. The exhibition space and shop, founded in the 1970s, are part of a national initiative to preserve this old tradition of Le Puy. This is a great place to witness the meticulous art of bobbin or spindle lace making, *dentelle aux fuseaux*, which once occupied much of Le Puy's female population. Some forty to fifty bobbins, each holding an individual thread, might be employed to work a single pattern.

Puy-de-Dôme

AMBERT

The Puy-de-Dôme region once counted numerous mills that churned out handmade paper between the fifteenth and nineteenth centuries. This off-the-beaten-track find is worth a detour to lay eyes on the last one still in operation.

PAPER

Moulin à Papier Musée Richard de Bas
04 73 82 03 11
www.richarddebas.fr

You need a lot of water to make handmade paper, and the rushing stream that runs alongside this five-hundred-year-old paper mill still does the trick. The interior is wet, too, but while the damp air and stone walls may chill visitors, the sight of hundreds of pieces of paper drip-drying across this vast mill delights the eye. The Moulin à Papier Musée Richard de Bas serves as a museum of paper-making techniques, as well as a working mill which crafts some two hundred to three hundred sheets of paper per day. In the shop, you can purchase small books, individual sheets of paper, and other beautiful paper treasures incorporating grasses and wildflowers.

THIERS

Today, 70 percent of the knives made in France come from Thiers. Unfortunately, industrial knife production eclipsed what began in the Middle Ages as a handmade tradition. Still, a trip to Thiers affords a fascinating tour of the French knife-making heritage. The town perches dramatically atop a cliff along the Durolle River, whose rushing waters once powered the grindstones that sharpened thousands of knife blades over the centuries.

Avoid the commercial shops along the aptly named rue de la Coutellerie, which display the works of Thiers's forty-odd industrial cutlery producers, as well as knives from other French centers, including Laguiole (page 148) and Opinel (page 127). Instead, head straight for the Maison des Coutelliers, associated with the museum, which seeks to preserve the artisanal heritage of the town's knife-making enterprises.

KNIVES

*Maison des Coutelliers
Musée de la Coutellerie
21–23 and 58 rue de la Coutellerie
04 73 80 58 86
www.musee-coutellerie-thiers.com

The sole purveyor of Thiers's artisanal cutlery tradition, the Maison des Coutelliers supports a handful of artisans who still produce knives using the old handmade traditions, with no mechanization. It's fascinating to watch these masters in action, using enormous grindstones to sharpen the blades. Museum exhibitions document the history of this craft, which once counted many women among its artisans.

BURGUNDY
(*Bourgogne*)

Côte d'Or

DIJON

GINGERBREAD

Mulot et Petitjean
13 place Bossuet
03 80 30 07 10
www.mulotpetitjean.fr

This fantastic emporium of Dijonnais specialties is famous for its *pain d'épices*, or gingerbread, stamped with the Mulot et Petitjean
logo. From the sumptuously decorated counter
of its store, founded in 1805, you can peer
into the *laboratoire* in the back and see the
pastry chefs at work. The *pain d'épices* sells for
between 5 and 25 euros and comes in plain
or different varieties with jelly and almonds.
Lovely gift baskets including *pain d'épices*, Dijon
mustard, and the town's famous liqueur, crème
de cassis, go for 20 to 30 euros.

MUSTARD

Maille
32 rue de la Liberté
03 80 30 41 02
www.maille.com

A mustard mecca, Maille dominates *moutarde
de Dijon* with its flagship store, in business in
this location since 1845. In the attractively
wood-paneled and glass-filled interior are
shelves lined with antique mustard pots, many
for display only. You can pick up a nice pot
commissioned especially for Maille and filled
with your favorite variety of its mustard for as
little as 22 euros, or spend up to 270 euros
for a large confection of its top-of-the-line
condiment. While other Dijon brands,
including Amora and Grey Poupon, have
been scooped up by multinational corporations, Maille continues its old tradition of
good Dijonnais mustard.

Nièvre

NEVERS

In the seventeenth and eighteenth centuries,
Nevers rivaled Rouen as one of France's most
important centers of faïence; today, a couple
of good artisans still produce the old patterns
and styles.

FAIENCE

*Faïencerie Montagnon
10 rue de la Porte-du-Croux
03 86 71 96 90
www.faience-montagnon.com

This is the best place in Nevers to purchase
quality reproductions of classic seventeenth-
and eighteenth-century designs. Montagnon
claims to be the oldest *faïencerie* in France,
founded in 1648; it is the last of the original
Nevers *faïenceries*, which numbered a dozen
around the time of the French Revolution.
Today, some twenty artisans work here,
making delicate tableware and Montagnon's
specialty—large-scale ewers depicting mythological subjects.

**Faïencerie d'Art de Nevers
François Bernard**
88 bis avenue Colbert
03 86 61 19 25
1 rue Sabatier
03 86 36 51 71
www.fayencerie-dart-de-nevers.com

François and Christine Bernard operate a
small retail shop on the rue Sabatier, and also
sell directly from their larger atelier on the
avenue Colbert, displaying their able reproductions of historical pieces of Nevers faience.

Musée Municipal Frédéric Blandin
Promenade des Remparts
03 86 71 67 90

The Blandin collection is the best place to
view historical Nevers faience from the sixteenth century onward. Hundreds of important pieces are displayed in the glass cases in
the Gothic chapter room of the old abbey of
Notre-Dame de Nevers. Call before visiting,
since as of this writing the museum was
undergoing a major renovation.

SAINT-AMAND-
EN-PUISAYE

The sober, sleepy town of Saint-Amand-en-
Puisaye stands at the center of an important
and centuries-old local tradition of utilitarian
pottery made with *grès*, an exceptionally
durable stone-based clay. You can spend an
enjoyable day popping in and out of the several dozen pottery shops, but don't miss those
listed below. NB: Due to its small size, the village does not have street-numbered addresses.

POTTERY

L'Attrape-Chien
Carrefour Carriès
03 86 26 24 82

Sabine Seguin runs this adorable wedge-
shaped boutique, the loveliest shop in Saint-
Amand. Tastefully exhibiting good, traditional
pieces, some of the best are original creations
inspired by pottery of the past.

Musée du Grès
Château de Saint-Amand
03 86 39 74 97

Alas, there's no museum shop, but this is a
great place to immerse yourself in the history
of the rustic pottery for which Saint-Amand-
en-Puisaye is known. Housed in a sixteenth-
century rose-brick château, the museum
chronicles this history in three exhibition
rooms.

*Espace Céramique Jacques-Jeanneney
Association de Sauvegarde du Patrimoine
Potier de Puisaye
Faubourg des Poteries
03 86 39 76 85

The best place in town to make a purchase,
this pottery cooperative occupies a row of cute
low-roofed cottages from which you might
expect the seven dwarves to emerge. These
miniature dwellings, comprising a courtyard
surrounded by stone farm buildings, display
the work of potters who belong to an association that promotes traditional local pottery.
An enormous nineteenth-century wood-fired
kiln dominates the space. Pots are arrayed in
the former three-room drying space, or
séchoir, as well as scattered on stumps and over
the grass in the courtyard and garden.

Poterie Nault
Route de Bitry
03 86 39 64 65

Perched on the edge of town, Poterie Nault, a
firm passed from father to daughter, displays
traditional, authentic pottery in a glass-front
studio. Its vast inventory spills out into the
garden and grassy lot.

CENTRE

Cher

BOURGES

Bourges is mostly known for its stunning Gothic cathedral, but it also holds one of France's least-known but best museums of artisanship.

GENERAL CRAFTS

*Musée des Meilleurs Ouvriers de France
Place Etienne Dolet
02 48 57 82 45

This great museum, across from Bourges cathedral, showcases the work of France's best artisans, who are selected triennially in a nationwide competition sponsored by the French ministry of culture. The designation Meilleur Ouvrier de France is one of the surest signs that an artisan ranks among the country's cream of the crop. The museum's first floor is dedicated to an annual temporary exhibition about one craft; past years have been dedicated to baskets, wrought-iron work, the arts of the table, and even hairstyling.

HUNTING HORNS

Franck Picard Musique
109 rue d'Auron
02 48 65 65 47

A master maker of wind instruments, Franck Picard has distinguished himself for carrying on a craft that is all but dead: the making of hunting horns, or *trompes de chasse*. Centuries ago, these brass wonders filled the woods with their ceremonious blasts. Monsieur Picard learned the craft from his father, and today collectors far and wide seek out his rare specialty.

LA BORNE

The village of La Borne and its surrounding countryside have become an artists' colony over the last fifty years, attracting potters from as far away as Scandinavia and Asia to experiment with different pottery techniques and more contemporary styles. Still, La Borne rests on a seven-century heritage of pottery making, and a couple of the town's artisans continue these traditions.

POTTERY

Centre de la Céramique
La Borne d'en Bas
02 48 26 96 21

This professional organization offers a good permanent exhibition of historical pottery from La Borne, displayed in an old school building. Some works are for sale in the tiny boutique.

Claude Gaget
On the road to Sancerre
02 48 26 95 71

Mainly a sculptor with a love for tree and plant forms, Claude Gaget has also distinguished himself as one of France's best creators of *sifflets*, or whistles, crafted in the form of animals, often birds or chickens. Collectors go crazy for these delightful objects, which were made in preindustrial societies around the globe.

Lulu Rozay
On the road to Henrichemont
02 48 26 73 76

Lulu Rozay is one of the town's most well-regarded craftspeople, creating the human figurines that have been made in La Borne for centuries. Her hallmark is women with bell-shaped skirts and fancy headdresses, whimsical and folkloristic portrayals that are highly collectible. Madame Rozay works from her evocative stone-and-brick home/atelier that epitomizes the bohemian atmosphere of La Borne.

Eure-et-Loire

CHARTRES

Southwest of Paris, the town of Chartres boasts France's most famous stained-glass windows in its early Gothic cathedral.

STAINED GLASS

Atelier Lorin
46 rue de la Tannerie
02 37 34 00 42
www.atelier-lorin.com

In business for 150 years, the Atelier Lorin is primarily a restorer of stained glass dating from the Middle Ages to the present day. The current proprietors, Gérard Hermet and Mireille Juteau, also create stained-glass panels on commission using the old techniques of leaded glass for which Chartres is world famous.

Galerie du Vitrail
17 rue du Cloître Notre Dame
02 37 36 10 03
www.galerie-du-vitrail.com

Whether you're seeking a quality antique example of stained glass or looking to commission a new piece, the Galerie du Vitrail is one of the best choices in France for its adherence to the traditions of this colorful medium. In its large galleries north of the cathedral, the Loire family exhibits works created here and in its ateliers outside of Chartres. For less than 20 euros you can pick up a small memento, or spend tens of thousands on a rare antique.

Indre-et-Loire

TOURS

In the heart of the Loire Valley, Tours previously rivaled Lyon as France's most prominent silk-production center. French kings brought Italian silk workers to the region to train local artisans and supply the royal families busily building lavish châteaux around the region.

The silk trade flourished until the French Revolution sent it into decline.

SILK

Manufacture des Trois Tours
35 quai Paul Bert
02 47 54 45 78
www.lemanach.fr

Alas, none of Tours's original silk works, or *soieries*, survive, but the Manufacture des Trois Tours inherited the tradition. Founded in 1829, this enterprise has supplied its celebrated fabrics for major state restoration projects, including the châteaux of Fontainebleau and Versailles. Unfortunately, this establishment is to the trade only, so it is not possible to visit its evocative *manufacture* filled with antique looms and pattern books. The good news: the company has a showroom in Paris under the name Georges Le Manach (chapter 1), where you can gaze upon—and buy—some of France's most luxurious and prestigious silks.

VILLAINES-LES-ROCHERS

This basket-making hub is located in a humid valley just a few miles south of the fairy-tale-perfect Loire Valley château of Azay-le-Rideau. Look for artisans working in below-street-level ateliers, where the humidity is ideal for keeping the willow reeds supple.

BASKETS

Coopérative Vannerie de Villaines
1 rue Cheneillère
02 47 45 43 03

A gigantic basket marks the entrance to this showroom and boutique of the Coopérative de Villaines, a professional organization representing some seventy basket makers in Villaines-les-Rochers. You can often witness the artisans at work, entwining reeds into objects of simple beauty.

GIEN

Collectors of Gien faience are some of the most zealous I know, and if you're one of them, you'll make a pilgrimage to this otherwise dreary town to find a bargain on some of France's best-known tableware.

FAIENCE

Société Nouvelle des Faïenciers de Gien
78 place de la Victoire
02 38 67 00 05
www.gien.com

This airy building houses the Gien empire, with a good museum and factory store. In the museum, you can learn more about the production techniques and view some of the most important historical pieces from this *manufacture* founded in 1821 by Englishman Thomas Hall. In the warehouselike factory store, you can find first- and second-quality Gien patterns priced about 25 percent below normal French retail prices. Many of the table services are close to mass produced, using a stencil method to apply color; for these, prices are lower. The nice *faïence d'art* collection, reproducing nineteenth-century designs in limited quantity, are painted by hand, and, naturally, cost more.

FRANCHE-COMTÉ

Jura

MOIRANS-EN-MONTAGNE

Brightly painted wooden toys bring cheer to the otherwise colorless town of Moirans-en-Montagne. In its shopwindows, you'll find miniscule turned wooden objects, from spinning tops to whistles, marionettes, and pots.

TOYS

Charliluce
59 avenue de Saint Claude
03 84 42 04 51
www.charliluce.com

Many French toy companies are headquartered in or around Moirans-en-Montagne, and most of the production is done on an industrial scale. Thankfully, Charliluce carries on the practice of turned wooden dolls and marionettes, painted in bright primary colors, some going for 200 to 300 euros. Today, the wood turning, or *tournage*, is accomplished by machine, but the rest is completed by hand.

Musée du Jouet
5 rue du Murgin
03 84 42 38 64
www.musée-du-jouet.com

This toy museum curates a collection of an astonishing sixteen thousand toys from France and around the world, documenting centuries of toy making with rotating exhibits. The shop carries an array of Jurassian toys in wood, metal, and plastic, many of them machine-made.

SAINT-CLAUDE

The center of French pipe making, Saint-Claude's businesses produce some two million pipes annually, destined for export and domestic sale. Obviously, the production is mainly industrial rather than artisanal, though a few true craftspeople quietly turn out tiny masterpieces. Most of today's pipe artisans import the roots of the fire-resistant *bruyère*, or briarwood, tree, already boiled and prepared, from North Africa or Corsica. Their professional organization, the Confrérie des Maîtres Pipiers de Saint-Claude, counts some of the world's most avid pipe aficionados among its members.

PIPES

Butz-Choquin
2 ter rue de Plan du Moulin
03 84 45 12 87
www.butzchoquin.com

Butz-Choquin turns out some 800,000 pipes per year, which are distributed around the globe. In spite of its mostly industrial production of briarwood pipes, a side of its business remains true to its artisanal roots. The company, which was begun in 1858, still crafts a limited number of fully handmade pipes each year, which are valued by collectors as true works of art.

Musée de la Pipe et du Diamant
1 place Jacques Faizat
03 84 45 17 00
www.musee-pipe-diamant.com

A rather hokey exhibition nonetheless displays some of the most interesting examples of historical pipes of Saint-Claude, including many carved with portrait heads of important people.

LIMOUSIN

Creuse

AUBUSSON

Unlike Beauvais (chapter 3) and Gobelins (chapter 1), the other big French tapestry centers, Aubusson is no longer a state-run tapestry maker. Luckily, a handful of individual *tapissiers* continue to weave these luxurious textiles here.

TAPESTRY

Atelier Robert Four
7 rue Madeleine
05 55 66 15 70
www.aubusson-manufacture.com

The factory and showroom of Robert Four are great places to witness the production of handmade tapestries. I have never seen more enormous hand looms, which require the coordinated work of many weavers. Robert Four also operates a fancy showroom on one of the most prestigious retail streets of Paris (chapter 1).

Manufacture Saint-Jean
3 rue Saint-Jean
05 55 66 10 08

The Manufacture Saint-Jean is one of the last historical tapestry enterprises in Aubusson, with a heritage that stretches back to the eighteenth century. Here you can witness the various stages of tapestry production, from dyeing (*teinture*) to weaving (*tissage*).

Musée Départemental de la Tapisserie
Avenue des Lissiers
05 55 83 08 30

This museum is a good place to start your foray into the history of Aubusson tapestry. The collection includes important works from the seventeenth century onward, as well as fascinating exhibitions of the preparatory drawings (maquettes) and patterns (*cartons*) used in the tapestry-making process.

Haute-Vienne

LIMOGES

Limoges is sprawling and not particularly charming, at least by French standards, yet it boasts a fantastic ceramics museum and several important historical monuments. The big-name porcelain makers who have made this town famous are located on the outskirts of town; you will need a car or taxi to get there. In town, there are a handful of good porcelain retailers on the boulevard Louis Blanc.

PORCELAIN

Ancienne Manufacture Royale de Limoges

Zone Artisanale du Moulin-Cheyroux
Aixe-sur-Vienne (outside Limoges)
05 55 70 44 98
www.manufacture-royale.com

It's worth the trek to Aixe-sur-Vienne, outside of Limoges, if you want to purchase the most traditional Limoges porcelain there is. This *faïencerie* began production in 1771, and a decade later it caught the eye of the French court. In 1784 it became a royal *manufacture* associated with the Manufacture Nationale de Sèvres (chapter 1) outside Paris. Today, the Ancienne Manufacture Royale still relies on delicate, fancy eighteenth-century reproductions as the mainstay of its collection, and its petite Limoges boxes are considered France's best.

*Bernardaud

27 rue Albert Thomas
05 55 10 55 50
www.bernardaud.fr

Located in an odd residential neighborhood on the outskirts of Limoges is Bernardaud's factory. The tour provides an education in the finer points of its processes, from molding to firing and decoration. The impressive production floor features shelves stacked to the ceiling with wares in various stages of completion. While molds (*moules*) are used to create many of the pieces, certain parts of the process are always done by hand, including adding gold rims and handles and fine painting. Between June and September, drop by anytime for a factory tour; during the rest of the year, call ahead to arrange a vist.

Haviland

40 avenue du Président John Kennedy (store)
05 55 30 21 86
Zone industrielle Nord, rue Philippe Lebon (factory)
05 55 04 73 00
www.haviland-limoges.com

You will see many of the fussy, fancy wares of Haviland in airport duty-free shops in Paris. The store on the industrial outskirts of Limoges serves as a museum displaying some of the unusual pieces of tableware created since its founding by American David Haviland. For me Haviland is a step down from the classier Bernardaud or the period pieces produced by Ancienne Manufacture Royale, but it boasts a loyal following among collectors.

Lachaniette
13 boulevard Louis Blanc
05 55 34 58 61

You simply can't go wrong here, as this retailer carries all the best French brands of *les arts de la table*—Bernardaud, Baccarat, Christofle, Daum, Raynaud, Puiforcat, Saint Louis, and others. If you don't have time to do factory tours or just want a beautifully wrapped gift, Lachaniette is a great one-stop shopping choice for France's top table arts. Across the street, a more unobtrusive Lachainette outlet is stacked high with factory seconds, or *deuxième choix*, from Haviland, Bernardaud, and others. You have to poke around the dusty shelves, but you may come away with a good deal.

Musée National Adrien Dubouché
8 bis place Winston Churchill
05 55 33 08 50
www.musee-adriendubouche.fr

This is one of the best ceramics museums in France (and I've probably seen them all). In a gracious old château, display cases highlight some of the most typical historical pieces from Limoges and elsewhere. A limited selection in the museum shop offers historical reproductions of Limoges porcelain, made by Ancienne Manufacture Royale.

Raynaud
14 ancienne route d'Aixe
05 55 01 77 55
www.raynaud.fr

Founded in 1925 and in its third generation of family ownership, Raynaud is still considered a relative newcomer to the Limoges porcelain scene. Raynaud offers a wide range of tableware styles, produced in great number but still very refined, using partly handmade techniques. Today, Raynaud is allied with Ercuis, a maker of some of France's most elegant silverware. In its factory store you can enjoy significant discounts.

RHÔNE-ALPES

Haute-Savoie

CHAMONIX-MONT BLANC

COWBELLS

Gérard Devouassoud
536 rue Vallot
04 50 53 04 88

Farmers throughout Haute-Savoie let their cows pasture in the fresh mountain fields. In order to keep track of their beasts, they attach to them large bronze bells on leather straps decorated in threads or metal studs with Alpine motifs like crosses and stars. The Devouassoud family has been forging these large *sonnettes* for more than a century. Gérard, in the fifth generation, is now passing on this skill to his son. Each bell is stamped with the Devouassoud name.

SAINT-JEAN-DE-MAURIENNE

Musée de l'Opinel
25 rue Jean Jaurès
04 79 64 04 78
www.opinel-musee.com

More or less machine-made since the beginning, these simple Alpine pocketknives are favorites for everyday use, with an unadorned wooden handle and a sharp blade. Joseph Opinel, the son of a toolmaker, designed this simple yet practical knife in the 1890s. Opinel knives are still highly valued and have become synonymous with this Alpine region. The trademark hand holding up three fingers, with a crown above, is a symbol of the cathedral of Saint-Jean-de-Maurienne. The museum boasts a large shop with a vast array of Opinel models. Today, the factory (located here as well) remains in the hands of the Opinel family.

GRENOBLE

GLOVES

Gants Notturno
10 rue Humbert II
04 76 46 56 60

The Notturno family traces its lineage to Naples, Italy, where a group of glove makers left in the nineteenth century to set up shop in Grenoble, then a prosperous glove-making city full of artisans. Today, it is one of the last families of this once-thriving trade. The atelier-boutique displays a representative selection of fancy leather gloves, some of which are destined for the Paris stage and cinema. You can pick up a pair for around 40 euros.

Rhône

LYON

I contend that Lyon is France's best-kept secret, holding attractions rivaled only by Paris—refined city living, world-class museums, some of the country's top restaurants, riverside walks, a charming medieval quarter—but without the tourists. Although its attractions are not always apparent at first glance, for those who take the time to discover and savor the pleasures of this special city, the rewards could not be greater.

GUIGNOLS

Le Guignol de Lyon
2 rue Louis Carrand
04 78 28 92 57
www.guignol-lyon.com

At the beginning of the nineteenth century, Laurent Mourguet, a former *canut*, or silk worker, made a career change. Inspired by the humorous characters from the popular Italian troupe the *commedia dell'arte*, Mourguet invented a puppet theater in Lyon with stories based around the travails of its funny main character, Guignol. For more than a century and a half, guignol theaters around town regaled Lyonnais audiences, but today,

Le Guignol de Lyon is one of the only venues for viewing this old local show. Here you can take a two-day course on making and animating marionettes, and purchase guignols ranging from 40 to 80 euros.

Musée Gadagne
1 place du petit Collège
04 72 56 74 06
www.museegadagne.com

The Musée Gadagne chronicles the history of Lyon with a special collection of vintage Lyonnais guignols, as well as puppets and marionettes from around the world. The museum and shop were undergoing renovation as of this writing; we hope for quality reproduction guignols in the new store.

JEWELRY

Joaillier Mickael K Designer
2 rue Saint Georges
04 78 42 07 29

The warm wood-beamed interior of this artisan jeweler's shop, in the heart of the artisan quarter of Vieux Lyon, invites passersby. You can observe the jewelers at work in the back of the shop, and admire the hammered silver pieces—updates of classical designs—in the front.

SILK

L'Atelier de Soierie
33 rue Romarin
04 72 07 97 83
www.atelierdesoierie.com

On long tables in this light-filled atelier near the place des Terreaux, artisans use engraved blocks to create patterns on plain white silk scarves. In the seventeenth century these blocks were made of wood, but today they are made of zinc. In the shop you can spend anywhere from 5 to more than 200 euros on a scarf, tie, handkerchief, and other small souvenirs. The atelier also produces works for another shop at 19 rue Saint Jean, which specializes in scarves and carries some products by the renowned silk maker Bianchini-Férier.

*Maison des Canuts
10–12 rue d'Ivry
04 78 28 62 04
www.maisondescanuts.com

This is the best place to understand Lyon's silk-making past. A friendly guided tour reveals rooms with enormous historic looms and images of the Lyonnais silk industry. You can also view a fascinating weaving demonstration and learn more about the Lyonnais silk workers (*canuts*) of the past. The shop carries handmade items woven here and elsewhere in Lyon, including scarves, ties, and fabrics by the yard, running between 15 and 150 euros.

Prelle
7 rue Barodet
04 72 10 11 40
www.prelle.com

Prelle is the heir to the grand old Lyonnais silk tradition. Though it now runs a modern factory, the company prides itself on continuing the handmade traditions, operating several giant old wood looms. With fancy showrooms

in Paris (page 41) and New York, its goods are expensive and made by custom order only. If you only want a small souvenir, head to the Maison des Canuts (see previous entry). For a special personalized treasure of interior decoration, though, Prelle is a top choice.

Soierie Saint Georges Ludovic de la Calle
11 rue Mourguet
04 72 40 25 13

Enter through the typically Lyonnais pink façade and wander into the recesses of this silk atelier, whose fantastic display includes a giant nineteenth-century loom and other antiques related to the silk trade. Lovely scarves and other silk fabrics hang alluringly around the shop, where prices range between 20 and 300 euros. You can also commission the artisans to create a custom design, which is much more expensive.

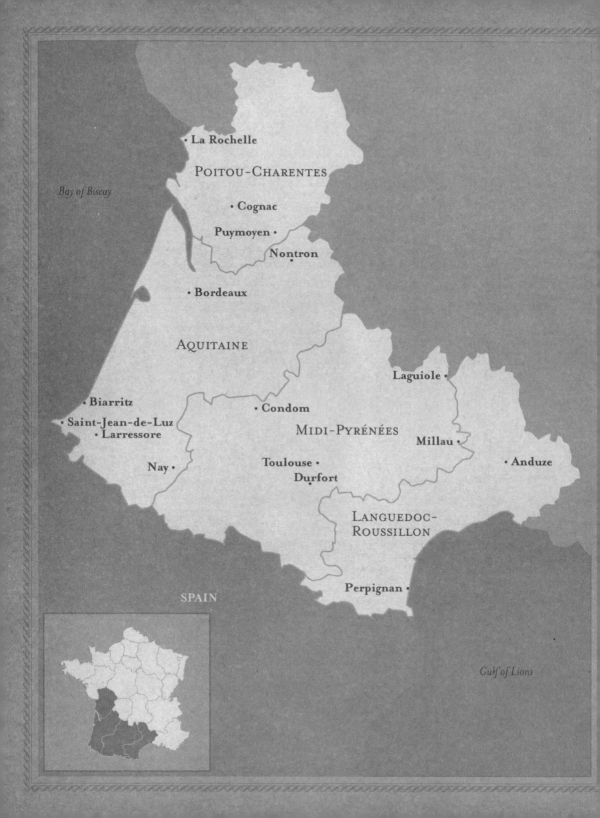

Bay of Biscay

• La Rochelle

POITOU-CHARENTES

• Cognac

Puymoyen •

Nontron

• Bordeaux

AQUITAINE

Laguiole •

• Biarritz

• Saint-Jean-de-Luz
• Larressore

• Condom

MIDI-PYRÉNÉES

Millau •

• Anduze

Nay •

Toulouse •
Durfort

LANGUEDOC-
ROUSSILLON

SPAIN

Perpignan •

Gulf of Lions

Chapter 5:

SOUTHWESTERN FRANCE

✦

F rance's most captivating area—that was my conclusion after spending a year walking the medieval pilgrimage routes to Santiago de Compostela and combing the small villages in southwestern France. This region—encompassing Aquitaine, Languedoc-Roussillon, Midi-Pyrénées, and Poitou-Charentes—is vast and diverse, with many cultural influences. Its ever-changing landscape descends into swamps and rises to snow-capped peaks; its cultural patchwork features copper pots, goose farms, bull-fighting, and a language that is not even close to French. You could spend the rest of your life in southwesten France and still not fully understand this area's complexities.

The southwest also boasts some of France's most treasured traditions, many culinary. In addition to a litany of artisanal cheeses that could fill a dictionary, the southwest is the locus for some of the country's greatest appellations—Cognac,

Armagnac, and Bordeaux. Foie gras, pâté made of goose or duck liver, is also associated with the southwest.

Historically, this region fiercely guarded its independence. It was one of the last areas to come under the authority of the French crown in the late Middle Ages, and therefore was the site of extensive medieval warfare against the "French," as locals called their invaders. The great medieval language of *Occitan,* or the *langue d'oc* (literally, "the western tongue"), the basis of many medieval romances and epic poetry, survives in regional dialects you still hear in the markets and the narrow streets of the southwest's villages.

That independent spirit thrives today in the Basque region that spans the Pyrenees, which still guards its ancient language, *Euskara,* a non-Indo-European tongue that is unrelated to French or Spanish. While most of the Basque culture resides on the Spanish side of the Pyrenees, the French Basques are closely linked to the language, history, culture, music, dance, and dress of their Spanish neighbors. Artisanally as well, the Basques uphold their own unique traditions, from the walking stick to the Basque cross, the espadrille, and even the beret.

THE TRADITIONS

ARMAGNAC AND COGNAC

A vigorous rivalry stands between the makers of France's most prestigious brandies, Armagnac and Cognac. Both stand as France's most celebrated spirits, or *eaux-de-vie,* and among its most interesting oenological traditions. Some of the region's best Armagnacs are turned out quietly by small, family-run operations that sell directly to visitors. In contrast, Cognac is the pride of some of France's most recognizable brand names: Rémy Martin, Martell, and Courvoisier. Both Armagnac and Cognac are prized *digestifs,* enjoyed in a brandy snifter whose unique shape releases and directs the prunelike aromas toward your nose. Sometimes used in cooking, they are often served alongside desserts.

No one knows when the amber-colored spirit called Armagnac was invented. Of course, proud residents of the Armagnac region boast that it began in their backyard long before a similarly produced spirit was ever invented in the town of

Cognac. Whatever its origins, Armagnac-producing grapes were cultivated in ancient Roman times; by the late Middle Ages, merchants were exporting the brandy to other parts of Europe. For centuries people extolled the medicinal properties and savory flavor of Armagnac, using it as a purported cure for red, itchy eyes, hepatitis, gout, and canker sores, and even healing skin wounds. Armagnac was also said to improve memory, and and was valued for its ability to preserve meats, fruits, herbs—even youth.

Although wines from the town of Cognac enjoyed bustling commerce in the medieval period—thanks to its location on the Charente River, which made transportation of the oak casks to the Netherlands and England a snap—the spirit Cognac as we know it was not developed until the early seventeenth century. At that time, winemakers began double-distilling wines, concentrating them for easier transport; drinkers in northern Europe would then dilute them with water upon their arrival. Thanks to the slow movement of merchant ships, people soon discovered that the *eau-de-vie* actually improved the longer it stayed in the barrel. Thus the spirit we now call Cognac was born.

Both Cognac and Armagnac have distinctly drawn geographical boundaries for grape production and distillation, a complex system regulated by the French government. The officially designated Cognac zone incorporates parts of the Charente, the Deux-Sèvres, and the Dordogne regions. Six growing areas, or *crus*, are designated in ascending quality from *bois ordinaires*, *bons bois*, *fins bois*, *borderies*, *petite champagne*, and finally, *grande champagne*, which is the finest (though it has nothing to do with the bubbly drink of the same name). The official production area of Armagnac is vast, covering areas of three administrative *départements*: the Gers, Landes, and Lot-et-Garonne. Each of the three official Armagnac zones—Bas-Armagnac, Armagnac-Tenarèze, and Haut-Armagnac—has a distinct type of soil and a mixture of up to ten grape varieties.

Armagnac and Cognac share a similar production process. Both begin with white grapes; *folie blanche*, *ugni blanc*, and *Colombard* varieties predominate, while up to seven additional ones are sometimes added in smaller quantities. However, the soil composition and microclimate are different between Cognac and Armagnac, which affects the taste and aroma of the grapes (even within each region, different growing zones have different soils). The grapes are harvested in the fall, and vinified, or turned into a basic white wine.

Next comes the distillation process, and it's here that the production of the two brandies diverges. The great copper stills or alembics—similar to the ones used to extract essential oils in the perfume-making process (chapter 6)—have evolved over the centuries, and each region proudly guards its own type. The *alambic armagnaçais* is a copper contraption with two distillation columns—sometimes on wheels to allow distillers to travel from winery to winery. The *alambic charentais*, for Cognac, is a more permanent fixture designed for double distillation. Producers may distill at their own estates, or bring the wine to a professional distillery or co-op. The copper alembics are important works of French artisanal tradition in themselves, crafted by hand and a product of completely local influence and origin. Government officials even regulate the design and measurement of these stills as part of the appellation process.

The colorless liquid that results from the distillation process is poured into oak casks, which are also works of artisanal importance—until recent times these giant barrels were completely crafted by hand. During the aging process, the brandy absorbs the flavors of the oak, so the unique characteristics of various species that grow in forests across southwestern France also influence the taste of the brandy.

Once the brandy has been sufficiently aged, the cellar master blends several brandies together; herein lies some of the regions' most carefully guarded secrets.

The blending, or *mariage*, process takes place to ensure consistency of taste and aroma from year to year from the same house. This is important for the large commercial producers with international brands, but smaller producers do not necessarily blend, which means that, like wine, their product varies from year to year.

Perhaps the biggest difference between the two brandies is the marketing budgets for each. Today, some six million bottles of Armagnac emerge from the region's approximately five thousand vintners, nearly half destined for export. By comparison, more than 90 percent of Cognac's 120 million bottles reach connoisseurs in the United States, Britain, Japan, and other parts of Asia. The larger Cognac houses even create particular blends and labels for specific foreign markets.

L ' O R I G I N A L

Here's how to read the labels: the designation always refers to the youngest brandy in the blend. Three stars, *trois étoiles*, or V.S. means that the youngest brandy has been aged two years. The designations V.O., V.S.O.P., and Réserve denote brandies that have been aged at least five years. The terms Extra, Napoléon, X.O., and Vieille Réserve signify that the product is at least six years old, and Hors d'Age means that it is at least ten years old.

Although Armagnac and Cognac mature nicely in the cask, unlike wine, once they are bottled, they do not improve with age.

Ç A   C O U T E   C O M B I E N ?

You will pay significantly less for brandy in France than in North America, especially if you buy directly from the producer. A bottle of Armagnac or Cognac from the year of a friend's birth makes a nice gift; the price corresponds to the rarity of the bottle, not to the quality.

C R È M E   D E   L A   C R È M E

Visits to Otard for Cognac (page 154), and to Ryst-Dupeyron for Armagnac (page 150) are personal favorites.

BERETS

Berets

No other fashion accessory is as typically French as the beret. This simple, round woolen hat ascended from the sheep pastures of the Basque countryside to international fame. The French army—and armies of other countries, too, for that matter—has even adopted the beret as an essential part of the uniform.

The beret originated in the Basque region of the Pyrenees and was worn by shepherds. The pure wool protected the shepherd from the elements, and the round, flat shape kept his head warm without obstructing his view. The characteristic hat became part of daily life in southwestern France: it's common to spot men wearing them while playing *boules* or strolling with their walking sticks, and children don them as part of their school uniforms. Up until the nineteenth century, berets were made by small-town artisans or even the shepherds themselves. At that time, the beret played a large role in forging a strong regional identity for this fiercely independent area. The industrial revolution propelled the manufacturing and distribution of berets across France and the world, though a handful of regional artisans still make them by hand.

Traditionally, the wool is knitted in a circular pattern, giving the hat its distinctive shape. The wool is made into felt by dipping the hat in soapy water, and then hammering it with wooden mallets so that the fibers meld together as tightly as the top of a billiard table. Finally, the beret is dyed. The traditional Basque beret was a natural tan, red, navy blue, or black, but today these authentic hats appear in a rainbow of colors. The highest-quality, most authentic Basque berets are made with virgin wool, which makes them water-resistant. The sweatband is made of leather, sewn into the beret.

Today, hat makers around the globe market products using the term "Basque beret," though the hat may have nothing to do with the Basque region. In reality, few berets are actually fashioned within the confines of the Basque territory anymore; some of the best beret makers are now concentrated in the neighboring region of Béarn. The Béarnais towns of Oloron and Nay are the center of authentic beret production today.

L'ORIGINAL

When purchasing a beret you must know two measurements: the size of your head, and the size of the beret you want. Opting for a tight or a floppy model is a matter of personal preference, rather than authenticity.

ÇA COUTE COMBIEN?

The price of the beret usually depends on the outer dimensions of it and not the size of your head. Prices for a good-quality, authentic French beret range from 20 to 100 euros, a bargain for a uniquely French item.

CRÈME DE LA CRÈME

The beret museum in Nay (page 145) includes a shop where you can get a good deal on an authentic beret, as well as learn more about the history and making of these hats.

BASQUE LINENS AND ESPADRILLES

Linge Basque et Espadrilles

 nce considered poor man's crafts, traditional Basque linens and espadrilles now enjoy an unparalleled vogue from home decor to haute couture.

Striped Basque linens, or *linge basque,* emerged from the simple country ways and poor economic conditions of the people in the region. Crafted at home, they were put to domestic use as table and house linens, curtains, aprons, tablecloths, and sheets, and special ones were displayed during festivals on the backs of oxen. These clean, simple country-house linens could not be further removed from the fancy embroideries of Paris or the luxurious silks of Lyon.

Using natural or white linens as a base, Basque weavers interlaced simple stripes, in natural tones or in deep red or green, the colors of the Basque flag. In recent decades, weavers have begun to introduce a wider variety of colors and patterns, though the traditional simple stripes still dominate both artisanal and industrial production. The Basque cross—the distinctive, swirly, four-armed symbol of the region—also appears on some linens. Today, much of the production of *linge basque* is done by machine.

Espadrille making, a related craft, also originated from the Basque country. As with Basque linens, its exact history is lost, but it seems that people have made this basic, low-cost footwear for a long time. The making of linen and canvas used in the espadrille uppers is linked with the tradition of *linge basque*. The roots of the word *espadrille* can be traced to the Provençal word *espardilho*, which refers to the rope or jute used to make the distinctive sole of the shoe. Long ago, people fashioned soles of rope or jute made from readily available natural materials. In the 1850s, a merchant from Mauléon, a small town in a rural Basque area known as La Soule, began to farm out the materials to *façonniers,* who sewed these shoes at home. By the end of the nineteenth century, electric sewing machines had mechanized the production, and the little zone of the Soule counted some thirty factories. These days, just a handful of companies produce quality, authentic Basque espadrilles.

L'ORIGINAL

You can buy espadrilles at every tourist trap, department store, and clothing boutique across the Basque region. However, many of these shoes have been machine-made in Asia and imported into France. If you want to ensure that you buy a Basque pair, buy directly from the artisan.

ÇA COUTE COMBIEN?

Espadrilles are an excellent value for a traditional craft. You'll rarely pay more than 100 euros for a top-of-the-line, made-to-order pair.

CRÈME DE LA CRÈME

Bayona (page 146) is considered one of the most authentic makers of traditional Basque espadrilles and still does much of the production by hand. Jean-Vier (page 146) puts a haute twist on simple Basque linens, operating several retail outlets across France.

GLOVES

Gants

Who would imagine that cheese and glove making would be linked? That's just what happened in Millau, in the eastern part of the Midi-Pyrénées. For many centuries, sheeps' milk was used in the production of Roquefort, the pungent cheese made in the same region. It's only natural that artisans would put the rest of the animal to good use later—*et voilà*, the glove-making industry was born.

A glove begins with the shorn, dried hide of a lamb, cow, or other animal. The huge sheep population in the Aveyron once provided an endless supply of raw materials for Millau's tanners. Many of today's *gantiers*, or glove makers, still use locally prepared hides from a *mégissier*, or hide preparer; others import prepared specialty hides from overseas. The raw hides are thoroughly cleaned to remove any impurities or fats, then moved to the tanning process. Tanning, the once-backbreaking process of preparing hides by treating them with tannins and other substances to make them supple and long-lasting, was a major industry in preindustrial Europe.

Between the seventeenth and eighteenth centuries, Millau's famous kid gloves became tied to the perfume industry. East of Millau in Provence, specialists around Grasse (page 160) were concocting essences from local jonquils, lavenders, and other flowers. The trades of the *parfumier* and *gantier* were closely linked from the late Middle Ages through the nineteenth century; fine ladies purchased kid gloves that were already infused with scent, and wore these elegant accessories nearly every day.

In the eighteenth and nineteenth centuries, many thousands of pairs of leather gloves issued from Millau's artisans, destined for fashion-conscious women all over Europe. Although many of the glove makers closed shop as more industrialized production moved to Asia, today Millau is still the self-proclaimed capital of *mégisserie*, the tanning of leather hides for making gloves and other items. Several important glove-making companies, including a few artisanal ones, remain clustered in Millau. Some of these enterprises cater to the haute-couture industry, while others supply niche markets like golf and cycling.

L ' O R I G I N A L

A high-quality pair of kid gloves from Millau will feel supple and buttery-soft, and should have a pleasant, natural leather smell, not a chemical one. Pick a pair off the shelf, or commission one of the excellent designers in town to fashion a one-of-a-kind pair.

Ç A   C O U T E   C O M B I E N ?

You can spend as little as 40 euros for a basic pair of leather gloves made in Millau, or up to several hundred for a custom pair. Look for pairs designed especially for golf, horseback riding, motorcycling, and more.

C R È M E   D E   L A   C R È M E

Lavabre Cadet (page 149) has created special couture gloves for Christian Dior and Yves Saint Laurent, and can make a custom pair for you on commission.

NONTRON AND LAGUIOLE KNIVES

Les Couteaux de Nontron et de Laguiole

I was first introduced to Nontron knives years ago in a country auberge in the Périgord, and for me it was a *coup de foudre*—love at first sight. Since then, I have been collecting these quality kitchen knives, distinctive for their rustic boxwood handles and their flashing steel blades.

The knife makers, or *coutelliers*, of Nontron have been respected for centuries. According to legend, a sword of the fifteenth-century king Charles VII was forged in Nontron. By the eighteenth century, there were some thirty-five knife makers in Nontron, but the industry declined with the dawn of the industrial age. The craft was nearly lost until the 1990s, when Coutellerie Nontronnaise, the oldest continuously operating knife company in France and the last artisanal knife maker in Nontron, decided to expand its production and marketing to save this important tradition.

At Coutellerie Nontronnaise, each knife is completely handmade by the same person from start to finish. The process begins with boxwood collected from the surrounding countryside, which is used to craft the distinctive handles. The artisans rely on old-fashioned woodworking tools, the same ones used for centuries— rasps, anvils, and other finishing tools. Knots or irregularities in the wood grain are part of the character of these rustic cutting implements, and they are left intact. Forged steel blades, tempered in river water, are inserted toward the end of the process, inscribed with a Nontron emblem. Nontron knives are crafted for specific uses, from knives for cutting steak and cheese to penknives and pocketknives.

Farther south in the Aveyron region is another important knife-making town whose artisanal tradition also survives thanks to the efforts of just one company—La Forge de Laguiole. Laguiole (pronounced "la-yull") is situated in a rural sheep-herding region, where shepherds had used a special knife for many centuries. In the 1830s, Pierre-Jean Calmels, the son of a local innkeeper, decided to transform this traditional knife into a folding model. The design caught on, but toward the end of the nineteenth century, it was subsumed by the more industrialized knife production of Thiers (page 119); by the 1930s, all artisanal knife production in Laguiole had ceased. Today, several industrial cutlery companies in Thiers (and some even in Asia) make "Laguiole" knives, but this refers only to the form of the knife and has little to do with the original handmade versions from Aveyron. It wasn't until the 1980s that the residents of Laguiole, with a push from a high-minded mayor, revived the old tradition of artisanal knives. Since the opening of

La Forge de Laguiole, other smaller artisanal enterprises have sprung up in town, but the quality has yet to catch up to La Forge de Laguiole.

Today, the classic knife handmade by La Forge de Laguiole has a slender, curvilinear design comprising a handle in horn or wood and a carved metal spine. Beyond this basic description, however, numerous factors will influence the price. The handles, for example, may originate from different parts of the horn of the Aubrac cow or other mountain animals; the tip of the horn is considered more desirable than the interior parts, both for its durability and beautiful veining. Some of the metal designs on the spine are made by machine, others by hand. Some of the blades may oxidize, while others do not. The metal spine usually has a mark, oftentimes a bee, but perhaps other designs. La Forge de Laguiole employs some of the region's best knife makers, including Virgilio Muñoz Caballero, who can only be called an artist; Caballero and others can even create a custom knife for you.

La Forge de Laguiole has engaged the services of some of France's top designers, including Philippe Starck, to develop a marvelous modern workshop and a special line of knives. The workshop produces some 300,000 knives a year, from standard steak knife sets to custom-made designs.

L'ORIGINAL

The origin and meaning of the enigmatic logo of Nontron—a horseshoe shape with three dots—is lost to history, but Coutellerie Nontronnaise continues to burn it on each wooden handle.

Most knives under the name "Laguiole"—sold in shops all over France—were not made in Laguiole, nor are they handmade. "Laguiole" has come to describe a type of knife, usually manufactured industrially in Thiers, or even in China. The best-quality, handmade versions are at La Forge de Laguiole, the company that has single-handedly revived the artisanal knife-making tradition in the town.

ÇA COUTE COMBIEN?

You can buy a good-quality basic knife from La Forge de Laguiole in the 50 to 100 euro range, but prices rise significantly for special models.

CRÈME DE LA CRÈME

To ensure you're paying for handmade quality, head directly to Coutellerie Nontronnaise (page 144) or La Forge de Laguiole (page 148). You can also buy these knives in Paris (page 40).

THE LISTINGS

AQUITAINE

Dordogne

NONTRON

Nontron seems to have been carved from the steep hillside on which it was built. It's here that knife artisans began crafting a particular type of knife in the fifteenth century. Today, just one enterprise upholds this centuries-old practice.

KNIVES

*Coutellerie Nontronnaise
33 rue Carnot
05 53 60 33 76
Place Paul Bert
05 53 56 01 55

La Guillaule, a blade company that helped revive Coutellerie Nontronnaise in the 1990s, provides the blades, but otherwise everything is as it was when the store began selling knives to locals in 1653. Up until 2000, just three knife makers toiled away in a space below the retail store. Today, a dozen artisans work down the street, each at their own station, in a more modern workshop designed by architect Luc Arsene-Henri, located on the place Paul Bert, with sweeping views down the road that leads to the valleys outside of town. Expect to pay as little as 20 euros for a small, simple model with the characteristic clog, carp tail, or ball handles; around 50 euros for a medium-size blade or Swiss army–style knife; or up to 3,000 euros for Nontron's fanciest model with an ivory handle.

Pyrénées-Atlantiques

BIARRITZ

Once a glamorous seaside playground for the rich and famous, Biarritz now appears as a faded *grande dame* still clinging to high-flying pretensions. Grand avenues sweep from the huge casino along the beaches, and high-rise hotels and many tourist traps front the water. Fortunately, there are a few places to pick up quality Basque crafts, although you'll pay more than in the region's less touristy inland towns.

BASQUE LINENS

Helena
33 rue Mazagran
05 59 24 06 23
27 avenue Edouard VII
05 59 24 73 43
www.helena-lingebasque.fr

The two Helena shops in Biarritz are excellent bets for finding high-quality, authentic Basque linens at a fair price. Until recently, when a larger company bought it, Helena was a family-run operation, and the firm still makes and sells its own brand of tasteful, crisp white linens with bright-patterned stripes. You can spend as little as 8 to 33 euros for bath or kitchen towels, and up to 75 euros for a beautiful tablecloth embellished with bright-colored stripes or the distinctive, swirly Basque cross. The store on the rue Mazagran is larger and offers a greater variety.

JEWELRY

Bijoux Rodon
1 rue Mazagran
05 59 24 74 30

It's hard to choose among the fun Basque-themed jewelry in this lovely, discreet shop. Pieces are created in the workshop outside of town on the way to Bidart, and worked in a variety of metals, with additional items in coral and diamonds. My favorites are the simple Basque-cross pendants hanging from a satin cord, but you can also find more ornate Basque-themed bracelets, rings, and earrings, reasonably priced between 35 and 150 euros.

LARRESSORE

A picture-perfect example of an old Basque village, Larressore boasts several inns and restaurants, as well as one of the most interesting artisans in France, Ainciart Bergara.

MAKILAS
(Basque walking sticks)

*Ainciart Bergara
Inthalatzia Bourg
05 59 93 03 05
www.makhila.com

One of the most fascinating artisan families in France, Bergara is the torchbearer of the Basque walking stick, the *makila* or *makhila*. The word literally means "to give death." Though it can be used as a lethal weapon if necessary, the Basque *makila* is a walking stick. It's also a collectors' item and an object of unparalleled craftsmanship. Collectors vie for these highly sought-after finds; a dealer might easily command thousands of euros for a well-preserved antique one.

The stick is documented as far back as the Middle Ages in connection with the pilgrimage roads to Santiago de Compostela, the paths that converged in the Basque country before crossing the Pyrenees into Spain. The *makila* maker selected a particularly strong and straight stick or branch of the slow-growing medlar tree, then put it in a furnace to dry the wood. The stick was then stained and straightened over a flame. At the bottom there is often a sleeve that, when removed, reveals a sharp blade of brass or steel, which transforms it from a cane to a weapon, to be wielded against animals or attackers. The sleeve itself is also often adorned with metal, engraved with decorative motifs from the Basque repertory. The handle is usually embellished with braided leather or, again, decorative metal.

Hanging from the rafters of the Bergara workshop is the raw wood that will be transformed into *makilas*, and everywhere there are sticks at different stages of production. Several workbenches are littered with tools (also handmade in this workshop) and on the walls are photographs of dignitaries who are proud owners of the elegant *makila*—including

Charles de Gaulle and Ronald Reagan—whose prized *makilas* are signed near the tip with the Bergara name. A symbol of respect and authority, Bergara's elegant walking sticks are prized within and outside of Basque culture.

If you stop in to learn about *makilas*, be prepared to stay awhile. Charles Bergara, born above this workshop, breathes passion into this ancient art, and vigorously shares it with visitors. The Bergaras work on commission only. A *makila* may take a week to six months to make and can cost from 250 to 1,000 euros. To devise the perfect one for you, the shop needs to know your height and weight. Remember that some *makilas* conceal a lethal blade, so don't plan to carry one on the plane home.

NAY

The Béarn region sits in the shadows of the Pyrenees, dotted with verdant valleys, winding roads, picturesque villages, black-and-white cows, and thousands of sheep. One of the most charming towns is Nay, home to museums showcasing two of France's most beloved icons of cultural patrimony: berets and foie gras.

BERETS

Musée du Beret
Place Saint-Roch
05 59 61 91 70
www.museeduberet.com

The arcaded town plaza hides a pretty courtyard that opens onto the Beret Museum, displaying the old hand-operated machines that still mold and stitch this traditional headgear. There is an excellent video with English subtitles that explains the process. The museum shop carries a good selection of traditional French berets in addition to imported hats. You can buy a basic, one-size-fits-all beret for 18 euros, regional variations like the traditional Bakarra model made in Nay for 28 euros, or a traditional Laulhère for 30 to 50 euros. On the higher-quality models, cap sizes are marked inside the band; you can have your head measured on-site if you're unsure.

BELLS

Jean Daban
24 rue des Pyrénées
05 59 61 00 41
www.daban.fr

If you've ever explored the Basque countryside on foot, no doubt you've enjoyed the symphony created by the clanging bells of herds of sheep as they move en masse from field to field. Jean Daban is the master of the ancient art of bellmaking, crafting these little *sonailles* from various metals with a special forge that reaches more than 1,000 degrees Celsius and renders perfectly formed ringers.

FOIE GRAS

Musée du Foie Gras
Pierre Laguilhon
177 rue des Pyrénées, Bénéjacq
05 59 61 90 90
www.laguilhon.fr

While you're in Nay, check out Pierre Laguilhon's foie gras museum, located on the traffic circle at the entrance to town, in Bénéjacq. Laguilhon began making foie gras at home years ago, and sold it door to door from his bicycle. Today, it is one of the southwest's best-loved varieties, and you will find it at supermarkets across France at slightly higher prices. This large, factory outlet–style building offers tastings along with Jurançon wine. The shop only sells the Pierre Laguilhon brand, made just behind the museum and store. You can sample the goods for free, as well as purchase individual jars of foie gras for as little as 15 euros or elaborate gift baskets for up to 75 euros.

SAINT-JEAN-DE-LUZ

A windy beach town with a relaxed attitude and many profitable ice-cream stands, Saint-Jean-de-Luz unfortunately has more than its share of tourists, and traps for them. The following are a few sellers of quality crafts.

ESPADRILLES

Bayona
60 rue Gambetta
05 59 26 05 40

You can't miss the six-foot-tall espadrille sculpture outside Bayona, considered one of the most authentic makers of the Basque espadrille for more than a century. The one-room boutique is stacked floor to ceiling with shoe boxes, but at least half its inventory spills out to the sidewalk stands. With a rainbow of colors to choose from, expect to pay 20 to 70 euros per pair. Look for the hand-stitching, which distinguishes these shoes from the machine-made versions scattered around town.

LINENS

*Jean-Vier, Ecomusée Tradition Basque
58 avenue Edouard VII
05 59 22 29 36
www.jean-vier.com

I would like to buy everything in this store! Jean-Vier, a hero of Basque culture who raised the time-honored, humble striped linens of the region to high art, has created a museum-like display of Basque life on the outskirts of Saint-Jean-de-Luz. Still, the main attractions here are the gorgeous, candy-striped house linens displayed throughout the rooms of this characteristic Basque farm building. You can spend as little as 4 euros for a hand towel, or up to a couple hundred euros for a large tablecloth, which pairs perfectly with dinner plates featuring Basque patterns.

LANGUEDOC-ROUSSILLON

Gard

ANDUZE

Enormous urns shaped like upside-down bells—referred to by the locals as *jarres*—have put the little town of Anduze on the map. Today, the handful of artisans in Anduze still use the local clay and hand-turn these large vases on huge potters' wheels. The style remains inspired by the classical past, using leaf swags and rosettes that recall the vases' Italian proto-types. The green, gold, and brown glazes impart a shiny finish that brings luster to many gardens and patios across southern France.

POTTERY

Les Enfants de Boisset
Route Saint-Jean-de-Gard
04 66 61 80 86

According to local lore, in 1610 a potter named Boisset saw an Italian vase at the market in Beaucaire and decided to replicate its classi-cal form and earthen tones. The result, repeated over and over today by artisans in this charming mountain village, was a large terra-cotta urn some three feet high, covered with brown and green glaze and decorated with gar-lands. Boisset is the descendant of the potter who began the tradition of Anduze *jarres*.

SAINT QUENTIN LA POTERIE

The name of this town could hardly be more fitting, for some two dozen potters operate studios here, with the best in town listed below. Strolling the alleys of this quiet village, you have the feeling that since ancient times, when locals began pulling clay from the earth to make utilitarian tableware, little has changed. You can take a look at the town's historic ceramic wares in the local pottery museum at the apex of the hill.

POTTERY

Isabelle Roger and Pierre Bernier
24 Grand'Rue
04 66 03 25 89

In a cavelike studio, this artisan duo turns out lovely multi-handled pots, platters, and special pitchers for water, wine, and olive oil. Their specialty is highly reflective glazes that make the dark blues and earth tones come alive.

Poterie Galtié
42 Grand'Rue
04 66 03 63 24
www.poteriegaltie.com

Patrick Galtié has created an inviting retail space (his large workshop lies outside of town) showcasing the best of his tableware, in unlikely colors ranging from yellow to pink. I fell for a pair of square platters, priced at 59 euros for a small one and 180 euros for a large one.

Pyrénées-Orientales

PERPIGNAN

I love Perpignan, a town that marches to the beat of its own drum. Here in the foothills of the Pyrenees and along the Mediterranean shores, you couldn't be farther away from Parisian wiles. Perpignan belies hints of Catalonia and the Basque country in its cuisine and architecture, as well as in its craft traditions, but it upholds a style all its own.

JEWELRY

Gil et Jean Barate
5 rue Louis-Blanc
04 68 34 37 68
www.gil-et-jean.com

Artisan jewelers Gil and Jean Barate specialize in red garnet jewelry, traditional in Perpignan and the surrounding area of Roussillon. In the eighteenth century, a special cut known as *taille Perpinya* made the town synonymous with this precious stone. Today, the Barates create reproductions of traditional regional jewelry with the stunning red stone, including crosses and other pieces.

LINENS

Maison Quinta
3 rue Grande des Fabriques
04 68 34 41 62
www.maison-quinta.com

A bazaar of Catalan culture and interior design, this vision of Françoise and Henri Quinta assembles some of the region's distinctive table and bed linens alongside furniture, tableware, and culinary products. Some of the items are handmade, but not all. Above all, come here to drink in the glorious colors and style of Perpignan and its region.

MIDI-PYRÉNÉES

Aveyron

LAGUIOLE

KNIVES

*La Forge de Laguiole
Route de l'Aubrac
05 65 48 43 34
www.forge-de-laguiole.com

A sleek glass and aluminum building designed by Philippe Starck houses the artisans crafting authentic Laguiole knives. This enterprise, founded in 1987, deserves a lot of credit for reviving a craft that had long since passed into industrial production in Thiers, wresting it back to its hometown and into the hands of able carvers.

MILLAU

In the 1960s, Millau employed more than six thousand people in the glove industry, and the town remains an important glove-making center. This long craft tradition can be documented back to the eleventh century, but may be even older.

GLOVES

L'Atelier du Gantier
21 rue Droite
05 65 60 81 50

More affordable than the couture gloves of Lavabre Cadet (see below), the quality creations of Christian and Chantal Canillac are lovely hand-stitched women's gloves starting at about 40 euros.

Lavabre Cadet
31 avenue Jean Jaurès
05 65 60 63 64
www.lavabrecadet.com

Give the artisans at Lavabre Cadet about two weeks, and they can turn out a custom-made pair of leather gloves to your specifications. Using luxuriously soft hides, this family of glovers has made accessories for Christian Dior, Givenchy, Yves Saint Laurent, and other French couture houses, under the rigorous eye of stylist Mary Beyer.

Maison Fabre
18-20 boulevard Gambetta
05 65 60 58 24
www.maisonfabre.com

Although you can buy Fabre gloves, bags, clothing, belts, and other leather goods at department stores in France as well as at Saks Fifth Avenue in the United States, you'll save a little by coming to the factory store. Fabre leans toward couture, with a collection of beautiful quality. If you're with a group, you can call in advance to arrange a factory visit.

Gers

CONDOM

Home to France's best producers of Armagnac, Condom and its environs are unwarrantedly overlooked. This small city, with its peaceful downtown and maze of winding streets, is surrounded by an astonishingly bountiful countryside of vineyards and sunflower farms. Visits to Armagnac producers are very different than those to the more trafficked Cognac producers. These are smaller, much more personal encounters, with real people whose success comes from the quality of their Armagnac and their hospitality—not from being associated with haute-couture impresarios, or from paying for the best international PR firm.

ARMAGNAC

Armagnac Janneau
50 avenue Aquitaine
05 62 28 24 77
www.janneau.net

Janneau is Condom's oldest producer of Armagnac, founded in 1851. Its aged estate carries a certain cachet (or *Janneau-sais-quoi*, as the owners cheekily claim). Of all the Armagnac producers, it is the only one that approaches Cognac's prestige. However, Janneau's vast on-site boutique remains a friendly, down-to-earth place to peruse antique alembics, special old bottles—each with a story—and the company's first account book. You can spend 16 to 38 euros for a nice bottle from the boutique. Call ahead to inquire about visits to the cellars; as of this writing, they were temporarily suspended due to renovations.

Armagnac Magnol
Domaine de la Brette
Route de Nérac
05 62 28 08 46
www.domaine-de-la-brette.com

This eighteenth-century estate on the outskirts of Condom is challenging to find but worth the adventure. Hillsides carpeted with sunflowers and grape vines lead the way to this producer of Armagnac, founded in 1963 and run by husband-and-wife team Johannes and Monique Gerzabek-Magnol. You can visit the cellars, or caves, and taste the fruits of this family's labor. The oldest bottles are ten years old and a bargain at just 25 euros. This is exactly the kind of mom-and-pop producer of Armagnac that makes exploring the region so much fun. You can even stay the night here, as the Gerzabek-Magnols run a bed and breakfast in their grand stone-walled estate.

Musée de l'Armagnac
2 rue Jules Ferry
05 62 28 47 17

The Armagnac museum does an excellent job of telling the story of the amber-colored spirit that put Condom on the map. There is a fascinating exhibit of copper alembics used for distillation that takes up the entire third floor. However, with so many interesting opportunities at the producers themselves, where you can learn about the Armagnac-making process, you may decide to skip the museum unless you have extra time.

Ryst-Dupeyron
Château Cugnac
05 62 28 08 08
www.ryst-dupeyron.com

Ryst-Dupeyron is the best-known maker of Armagnac, and one of the oldest, founded in 1905. Its headquarters occupies a fortresslike château in the center of Condom, with a chilly aging cellar redolent with atmosphere and the heady fumes of *eau-de-vie*. In the store you can spend as little as 19 euros for a V.S.O.P. bottle, or up to 160 euros for a special forty-year-old bottle. It offers an excellent tour of its museum and distillery in English, Spanish, and German, with tastings included.

*Armagnac Larressingle
Château de Larressingle
05 62 28 15 33
www.armagnac-larressingle.com

For a special and personalized visit to an Armagnac maker, head straight to Larressingle. For five generations, the Papelorey family has presided over the château of Larressingle, surrounded by its prized vineyards. Chances are the cellar master himself will welcome you into his cozy *laboratoire* to witness the alchemy involved in blending *eaux-de-vie* to produce a distinctive flavor that becomes the house's own brand. Larressingle is located in the city center, tucked along the far side of the river. In the shop you can purchase a nice bottle of V.S.O.P. for 15 to 35 euros, or an X.O. for around 30 euros.

Domaine de Cazeaux
Route de Nerac, Lannes
05 53 65 73 03
www.domaine-cazeaux.com

The affable proprietor, Eric Kauffer, welcomes you to the Domaine de Cazeaux in Lannes, outside Condom. This family Armagnac producer is worth the effort to locate for its delightful country estate and friendly cellar tour. A centuries-old stone house serves as the sampling room and store selling reasonably priced Armagnacs. You can buy a five-year-old vintage for 19 euros, or walk away with a bottle of the house wine for a mere 3 euros.

Haute-Garonne

TOULOUSE

Toulouse is a great shopping and strolling town that boasts many opportunities to sample its culinary specialties; unfortunately, there are few old-fashioned artisans accessible to visitors in the city center.

LINENS

Jean-Vier
24 rue Rémusat
05 61 21 27 42
www.jeanvierparis.fr

Occupying prime real estate on one of Toulouse's nicest shopping streets, this branch of Jean-Vier, one of my favorite table-linen makers in France, offers bath towels from 45 euros, tablecloths for around 100 euros, and fabric by the meter. The display is clean and smartly organized, though with a more limited selection of brightly striped table linens than that of its larger stores in the Basque country.

VIOLETS

Péniche Maison de la Violette
Canal du Midi
05 61 99 01 30
www.maisondelaviolette.fr

The aroma of violets hits you long before you actually see the boat named *Vulcain* docked in Toulouse's Canal du Midi, near the train station. This is a unique shopping experience, a floating "barge-boutique" that specializes in products made with local violets. Its creator, Hélène Vie, is credited with reviving the production of violets in Toulouse in the 1970s. Here you can purchase everything you could possibly conceive of made with violets, including candy, honey, herbal teas, dolls, baskets, flowering violet plants, and candles, all at reasonable prices.

Tarn

DURFORT

Durfort bills itself as France's copper capital, but unfortunately the craft tradition that once dominated this sleepy village is all but dead. Europe's last functioning *martinet*—a large water mill-powered block of stone that hammers copper sheets—still operated in Durfort until recently, but alas, was finally retired. The only workshop creating copperwares by hand in Durfort today uses prefabricated sheets, as few are willing to pay the high labor costs involved in producing handmade copper. Many shops in Durfort still sell copper to unwitting tourists, but be aware that most of it has been worked in Morocco and imported. Scores of German and English travelers are dutifully bused to Durfort's central square, but with the few exceptions listed below, the town has been sadly reduced to little more than a tourist trap for copper buyers. Fortunately, a few other enterprises in town are more promising for shoppers of other crafts, including baskets.

BASKETS

Atelier de Vannerie Française
Route de Revel
05 63 50 82 63

When you enter this simple, modern building with its large sign luring passersby, you'll likely find the husband-and-wife basket-weaving team of Bernard and Brigitte Gendre doing what they do best: creating lovely hand-woven baskets. Not only do they craft baskets, but they actually grow the reeds and grasses they use in their production. Working cross-legged on their near-floor-level workbench, they create picnic baskets, baby bassinets, room screens, and bread baskets, ranging in price from 30 to 500 euros.

COPPER

Musée de Cuivre
Le Plo
05 63 74 22 77

The municipality of Durfort organizes a large exhibition space where you can view antique copper-working tools and wares on loan from various Durfort residents, many of whom count copper artisans in their family trees. A video shows the workings of the town's old *martinet*—the stone hammer that beat copper into sheets for Durfort artisans for centuries. The entrance to the museum is in the rear of the building, next to the post office.

Pierre Vergnes
5 Le Plo
05 63 74 10 52
www.pierrevergnes.com

You have to hand it to Pierre Vergnes for being the last true authentic copperware maker in Durfort. Vergnes operates two shops, the larger at 5 Le Plo, and a smaller boutique across the plaza on a little street called Le Bourg. Both shops carry similar merchandise, but at Le Plo you can watch the copper artisans at work. You'll hear the din of hammering long before you see a half dozen men pounding away at copper vessels, using hammers of different sizes and designs, in the large workshop attached to the store. Even Vergnes resells some imported copper in his shop, so look for the "PV" logo to ensure you're buying vessels made on the premises.

LEATHER

Crys Parker Creations
11 Le Plo
05 63 74 19 52

While most of the items in this store are produced elsewhere, Crys Parker runs an active in-house, custom-order business in leather clothing and bags. The energetic Parker, who works alongside his father, welcomes your sketches and has made a specialty of creating eccentric leather coats with loud colors and fur accents. You can buy a simple wallet for 29 euros, a Crys Parker bag for around 170 euros, and a custom-made leather jacket for up to 2,000 euros.

POITOU-CHARENTES

Charente

PUYMOYEN

PAPER

Moulin du Verger de Puymoyen
05 45 61 10 38
www.moulinduverger.com

Historical documents attest to this paper mill's existence, south of Angoulême, as far back as 1537. Over the course of the next three centuries, Moulin du Verger was just one of many paper makers in this area of Poitou; today, it's among the last remaining mills of its kind in France. A tour leads you through the dank, cavernous stone-walled rooms where paper artisans start with old rags, create a paste, color it with vegetable dyes, press it into sheets, and hang it up to dry on clotheslinelike hangers made for that purpose. In the store, you can buy beautiful marbelized papers and reproductions of old sheafs from the fourteenth to the nineteenth centuries.

Charente-Maritime

COGNAC

Cognac is well organized for the many thousands of tourists who flock here to visit the famous makers Otard, Rémy Martin, Martell, Hennessy, and Courvoisier, as well as smaller producers. Otard, Hennessy, and Martell stand in the city center, within walking distance of one another; Rémy Martin and Courvoisier are on the outskirts of town. The tours are similar; each explains the agricultural particularities of

the region and the distillation process. All, with the exception of Courvoisier, offer paid tastings with the visit. A black fungus that thrives on the vapors used in Cognac production blackens the inside cellar walls of all the producers where the brandy ages in oak casks. It also soils the town's façades, though on a recent trip the city was significantly cleaned up—a massive municipal effort, no doubt.

CASKS

Seguin-Moreau
Zone industrielle, Merpins
05 45 82 62 22
www.seguin-moreau.fr

Each year this enterprise creates some fifty thousand *barriques*—the oak casks used to age Cognac—yet a large part of its techniques remain artisanal. Starting with planks from hundred-year-old oak trees, Jacky Allary and his team season the wood, then mold thirty-two planks to form the classic Cognac barrel, encircling it with metal bands. A complex process of hammering and flame-seasoning ensures that each barrel is watertight and ready to flavor each batch of Cognac.

COGNAC

Hennessy
Quai Hennessy
05 45 35 72 68
www.hennessy-cognac.com;
www.hennessy.com; www.hennessy.fr

A ferry boat transports you to the grand facilities of Hennessy along the Charente River, just as barrels of Cognac have been conveyed for more than two centuries. Richard Hennessy, an Irishman and former mercenary, founded this enterprise in 1765. The cellar tour ends in a sleek boutique, in a contemporary building designed to complement the old facilities next door. At a long bar, you can sample a range of Hennessy products—the most expensive of all the big-name Cognacs. The quality and quantity of what you sample depends on how much you pay for the tour. Today, the brandy is part of the LVHC group that includes Louis Vuitton and Chanel—the "H" stands for Hennessy.

*Otard
Château de Cognac
127 boulevard Denfert-Rochereau
05 45 36 88 88
www.otard.com

I think this is the most interesting tour in Cognac, as much for its castle as for its cellars. Baron Otard bought this medieval fortress in 1795 with the intention of making Cognac. The ramshackle building has been fixed up—just a little—since then, and your jaw will drop as you wander through its dark chambers and thick-walled passageways. Eventually your guide, dressed in a medieval costume, will turn to the process of Cognac making, and the tour ends in the vast, shiny-floored boutique. There you can spend anywhere from 28 to 100 euros

for a bottle of house Cognac, and ponder bottles marketed specifically to the American and Asian markets.

La Cognathèque
8 place Jean-Monnet
05 45 82 43 31
www.cognatheque.com

La Cognathèque is a good place to start your visit if you don't know much about Cognac. This friendly family store stocks some three hundred different Cognacs in smart, bright displays. The helpful staff can provide a quick education about the different grades, and the nuances of any brand that interests you. They have a soft spot for small, local producers and carry a nice selection of their bottles. But they also have an impressive collection of big names for collectors—some very expensive stuff. You can spend anywhere from 20 euros for a standard V.S.O.P., or up to 5,000 euros for a Courvoisier in a Baccarat crystal bottle.

Martell
7 place Edouard Martell
05 45 36 33 33
www.martell.com

The oldest, most attractive, and least snooty of the big-name Cognac houses, Martell is worth a stop. Entering the ornate gate to the cobblestoned courtyard, you can visit the home of the founder, Jean Martell, exhibiting personal effects such as his hat, pipe, books, and letters. Fortunately, the guides don't drag out this part too long, and soon enough you get to the Cognac cellars, where the type of tasting you can enjoy depends on your tour package. For me, the most interesting part is a visit to the cooperage, or barrel-making operation. Here you can get a feel for the impressive craftsmanship that goes into the making of the oak casks for aging Cognac—from the cutting of staves to the metalsmithing involved in making the bands that hold them together. In the shop you can spend anywhere from 18 to more than 1,000 euros for Martell's various grades of Cognac.

Rémy Martin
20 rue de la Société Vinicole
05 45 35 76 66
www.remy.com

For thirty years, Pierrete Trichet has held
the distinction of being the only female
cellar master in Cognac. Right from the start,
Rémy Martin sets out to do things a little
differently, and it is proud of its innovative,
modern image. Its estate lies fifteen minutes
outside of Cognac. The large, trendy bar
features contemporary orange couches,
making you feel as if you are in a New York
club. The tour includes a train ride around
the property and vineyards, as well as a visit
to its three-level cellars. The store has good
values for the quality, and you can spend
20 to 1,000 euros on various qualities
of Cognac.

Courvoisier
Place du Château, Jarnac
05 45 35 55 55
www.courvoisier.com

Jarnac, a few miles east of Cognac, is home
to the Courvoisier dynasty, today owned by
the American multinational company Fortune
Brands. Visitors to this modern riverside
building go home with a mini-bottle of
Courvoisier V.S.O.P. However, there are
no cellars here, so unless you have lots of
time and money or are a die-hard Courvoisier
fan, opt to tour one of the other producers,
as this is a potentially expensive visit without
much soul.

LA ROCHELLE

Part historic maritime city, part beach town,
La Rochelle is full of life and visitors eager to
take in the delights of its castle, private yachts,
cafés, aquarium—and a few unique artisans,
one of which follows.

MARITIME KNIVES

Farol
64 quai Louis Prunier
05 46 50 53 05
www.farol.fr

Farol specializes in handmade knives for
maritime use, with a signature whale-shaped
handle. Part of the Musée Maritime complex
behind the aquarium, the workshop occupies
a low-slung complex that was once part of the
loading docks and fish market. Walking into
the Farol workshop is like being inside a
barge, and the knives are beautiful in their
pure simplicity. Two cases display knives
ranging in price from 5 to 30 euros, and up
to 230 euros for a carving knife. Farol makes
just four thousand pieces per year, each one
by hand. This is a find, especially for boaters
and fans of maritime treasures.

ITALY

PROVENCE–ALPES–CÔTE
D'AZUR

· Avignon
· L'Isle sur la Sorgue
· Saint-Rémy-de-Provence
·Tarascon

· Arles

· Manosque
· Moustiers-Sainte-Marie
· Riez

· Salon-de-Provence
· Gréoux-les-Bains

· Salernes
· Tourrettes-sur-Loup
· Aix-en-Provence
Saint-Paul-de-Vence
Grasse · · Nice
· Valbonne
Biot ·
· Aubagne
Cannes· Vallauris

Marseille

Cogolin · · Saint-Tropez

Mediterranean Sea

Chapter 6

SOUTHEASTERN FRANCE

❦

I will never forget my first view of Provence, which I glimpsed from a train window as a teenager traveling from Lyon south to soak up the landscape made famous by Vincent van Gogh. My train rumbled steadily as a landscape of stubbly bushes and ragged patches of haphazardly organized crops rose and fell on either side. The groan of the train sent a herd of newly shorn sheep darting up the crest of a hill, the sun making flickering patterns on their saggy skin as they moved in panicked unison toward a poppy field. Suddenly, red-tiled rooftops appeared like a shimmering mirage through the afternoon haze, crouching around the tired-looking Baroque façade of an otherwise austere parish church, like a venerable *grande dame* whose severe demeanor is grotesquely enlivened by overapplied cosmetics.

I'm not the only person who has been seduced by this glorious region, with its Mediterranean colors, warm fields of lavender and sunflowers, and alluring architecture. You may travel to this magic land, only to discover yourself elbowing for space among thousands of American, English, German, and Japanese tourists, all vying for their own little piece of paradise. It seems that everyone wants to inhale the colors and flavors of Provence, from its lavender-scented linens to its shimmering olive groves and Mediterreanean feasts.

Although there are no longer any secrets in Provence, thanks to its popularity, the region's pleasures are still real, and its artisanal traditions are some of the most special in France. Some of its typical products center around culinary and olfactory pleasures—jams, honey, sweets, and condiments—plus anything you can imagine made with olives, from tapenade to soaps, lotions, and bowls crafted of olive wood. All of these treats are beautifully displayed on characteristic Provençal tables set with bright, happy pottery and sunny-patterned tablecloths handspun across the region.

Provence will always be Provence, no matter how overrun. Go in the off-season, slow your pace, keep your sense of humor, and enjoy.

THE TRADITIONS

BUBBLED GLASS

Verre bullé

Visitors flock from far and wide to Biot for its bubbled glassware, *verre bullé*. This happy colored glass is already famous in the United States, thanks to Pierre Deux catalogues, where it is usually flaunted on colorful Provençal table linens.

Verre bullé is a relatively recent craft in Biot. Once upon a time there were many traditional glassblowers across Provence, but the craft declined and by the nineteenth century most had closed shop. In the 1950s, Eloi Monod, who was eventually elected mayor of Biot, had the idea to found a glassblowing enterprise in his hometown in the hills above Nice, and he attracted important glass artists to a large studio. The opening of the Fernand Léger museum, just a stone's throw away, brought heightened interest to the area as an arts center.

The artisans in Biot became known for *verre bullé*, which they create by adding sodium carbonate to the paste into which they dip their blowpipe. The bubbles

become trapped as the glass is blown, forever reflecting light and creating a beautiful surface for this fragile art.

Today, with the popularity of French country and "shabby chic," this rustic and colorful glass has enjoyed renewed popularity. Beyond Biot, other glass artisans across the region have revived this craft, hoping to cash in on its popularity with the hordes of French and international visitors to the Côte d'Azur.

L ' O R I G I N A L

Actually, Biot's most authentic craft tradition is not glass at all, but the large terra-cotta urns called *jarres* that Ligurian immigrants began making here in the Middle Ages. These huge terra-cotta containers, transported on ships, garnered a reputation across the Mediterranean for their durability and ability to preserve olives, oils, and other food products.

Ç A   C O U T E   C O M B I E N ?

A set of four *verre bullé* glasses will set you back around 100 euros, and don't forget to add the cost of shipping and insurance for these fragile items.

C R È M E   D E   L A   C R È M E

Watching artisans at La Verrerie de Biot (page 173) will give you a quick education in glassblowing. For traditional Biot pottery, go to La Poterie Provençale (page 173).

P E R F U M E

Parfum

 rasse, north of Cannes, was first mentioned in historical documents in the Middle Ages. At that time, its tanneries—then its main industry—clustered around the town square, the place aux Aires. In the fields surrounding Grasse, the tanners also cultivated flowers and plants used to cure and dye the animal hides that were utilized for making gloves and other leather goods. Out of this now-defunct industry grew a new one—perfume—that would put Grasse on the map.

Though it may seem strange, originally glove and perfume making were inseparable. As early as the medieval period, noble ladies purchased calfskin or lambskin gloves

imbued with scent, so it's not surprising that the tanners evolved into perfume makers. By the early eighteenth century, however, the perfumers had separated from the tanners' guild to form their own trade group, and they began to grow jasmine, roses, and other flowers that they combined in fragrances that were all the rage during that era. Notably, Grasse's most famous native son, the eighteenth-century painter Jean-Honoré Fragonard, was the son of a *gantier*, a glove maker closely linked to the perfume trade.

Known as the "balcony of the Riviera" because of its amphitheaterlike topography overlooking fields of flowers and the Mediterranean Sea, about five and a half miles distant, Grasse hosts a microclimate perfectly adapted to growing the delicate flowers key to perfume production: jasmine, roses, jonquils, carnations, orange blossoms, lavender, and violets. Grasse's perfumers reaped these blooms and developed many of the techniques still employed in perfume production. The city remains important in processing the raw materials for the industry today.

The art of creating a scent begins with harvesting the many thousands of flowers it takes to yield just a small volume of perfume. The first stage of production is a treatment with animal fats. This is accomplished with a process called *enfleurage*, in which fresh flowers are placed on a layer of lard and stacked in glass trays, so that the flowers impart their scent to the fatty material. Alternatively, some perfumers put the petals into hot water with lard, then filter the flowers out, leaving the fat impregnated with the fragrance. Next, the lard is frozen, filtered, and concentrated into a liquid.

The second step in the process is distillation. In this stage, the concentrate is processed with a copper still, the same type of contraption used to distill spirits like Cognac and Armagnac (chapter 5). The resulting product is the flowers' essential oil. In the final step, extraction, the essential oils are mixed with solvents to produce a pure scent. In this process, a talented "nose" with a highly attuned sense of smell blends as many as several hundred essences to create a one-of-a-kind fragrance.

Today, many companies in Grasse work behind the scenes of the perfume industry, acting as wholesalers and processing the raw materials. Many of the essential oils extracted in Grasse are transformed into famous brands for Guerlain, Dior, and other couture houses. Three perfume houses in Grasse are accessible to visitors: Fragonard, Galimard, and Molinard. Be sure to take one of the free tours at these establishments, and don't miss the museums—a great education in the perfume-making process awaits.

L'ORIGINAL
Though the flowers around Grasse only constitute a small fraction of those used in today's perfume production, its jasmine is still highly prized. It takes 8,000 jasmine flowers to make just two pounds of perfume. Provence supplies some 80 percent of the world's lavender, which is used in numerous perfumes and beauty products.

ÇA COUTE COMBIEN?
Perfume in Grasse is a relative bargain, even compared to the duty-free shops. I suggest you buy one of the scents from Grasse's three big makers for a unique souvenir.

CRÈME DE LA CRÈME
Of the three perfume makers in Grasse today, my favorite is Fragonard (page 175).

PROVENÇAL FABRICS
Indiennes

 unny Provence conjures images of bright cotton fabrics in gold, blue, and green, lively prints that adorn tabletops, windows, and even hardy Provençal women. These so-called *indiennes* became popular in the seventeenth century, when the French began importing vividly printed fabrics from India into the port cities of Provence. The French emulated these happy patterns, and homespun *indiennes* captured the region's warm spirit. For special occasions, women began topstitching and quilting the paisleys and swirls that char-

acterize the designs to give them even more dimension. These lovely topstitched linens, or *piqués*, evolved into one of the most characteristic crafts of Provence. Denim (literally, *de Nîmes*) also arose from the popularity of light cotton fabrics.

Traditionally, woodblocks dipped in special dyes were used to print patterns on these light fabrics. These woodblocks were also works of artisanship, as the designs had to be carved in reverse to make a print. Virtually all of the companies making *indiennes* today use screen-printing techniques to make the designs. However, all over Provence you can find pieces of exquisite beauty that are still topstitched by hand, an incredibly painstaking task. Bed and table linens with handworked parts are a lovely regional souvenir.

One of the most beautiful and typical Provençal linens you can buy is a *boutis*, or quilted bed coverlet. *Boutis* is an old Provençal word meaning "to push," as in to push a needle to create a design. *Boutis* are usually made of cotton, but you may also find them in silk or wool. Thin muslin is used as stuffing, and then the patterns are worked with topstitching. Some women use a chalk design pricked with little holes as a template, which is removed once the stitching is complete. *Boutis* are traditional Provençal wedding gifts and were highly prized family treasures in centuries past.

These days, two Provençal companies, Souleiado and Les Olivades, dominate the production and marketing of *indiennes*. These companies, both founded only in the twentieth century, closely follow the historical traditions. Souleiado and later, Les Olivades, found success in North America under the brand name Pierre Deux, spreading old Provençal style throughout the world.

L'ORIGINAL

Most of the tablecloths, bedcovers, placemats, napkins, and other Provençal textiles you see in tourist shops are entirely machine-made and vary vastly in quality. Carefully examine the stitching: machine stitches are regular and even, while pieces that are topstitched by hand bear the marks of human imperfection and irregularity. Some of the most valued pieces are antique hand-stitched *boutis*, which you can find among certain well-regarded dealers.

ÇA COUTE COMBIEN?

You can find a quality *piqué* cushion cover starting at around 30 euros, or pay up to 500 euros for a *boutis* you can use as a full-size bedcover. Antique or special ones will cost more.

CRÈME DE LA CRÈME
While Souleiado and Les Olivades make home decor, Mistral (page 186) has revived century-old designs into fashionable clothes. Connoisseurs will appreciate the collection of antique *boutis* at Michel Biehn (page 187).

POTTERY AND FAIENCE

Poterie et Faïence

I challenge you to find a single Provençal village that does not have at least one ceramics studio. The craft has been ubiquitous in the region since ancient times. In spite of its omnipresence, artisans tend to cluster in several spots across Provence, including Vallauris, for utilitarian pottery; Salernes, for architectural and decorative tiles; and Moustiers-Sainte-Marie, for refined faience.

Moustiers-Sainte-Marie, in a craggy landscape of northern Provence known as Les Gorges du Verdon, is probably the most renowned of the region's ceramics centers, if not all of France. According to legend, a certain Pierre Clérissy learned how to make faience from an Italian monk at the Servite monastery in Moustiers. In the 1670s, he founded a *faïencerie* there, and over the next century its wares became known for their fancy decorations of garlands, flowers, and grotesques against a translucent white background.

By the French Revolution, there were 2,500 inhabitants in Moustiers—nearly four times as many as there are today—and half of them worked in the ceramics industry. Entire generations of families staked their fortunes on faience and created many thousands of fancy wares decorated with the hallmarks of these leading names.

One of the reasons for the emergence of the faience tradition in Moustiers is the abundance of clay in the craggy gorges surrounding the town. Much as in the past, today's *faïenciers* crush, purify, and strain this ruddy material in basins, then dry and bake it. The clay is put in humid caves and beaten to eliminate any air pockets. After shaping vessels on a potter's wheel or forming them with molds (*moules*), they are stacked and put in a kiln at 1,000 degrees Celsius. Originally, this was done over an open fire in a specially built room; workers adjusted the number of bricks blocking the door and controlled the temperature by reading the color of the flame. These days virtually all of the artisans in Moustiers rely on electric kilns. Thirty to thirty-six hours later, the pieces emerge an ashy-colored biscuit.

After cooling for twenty-four hours, the pieces are washed in an enamel bath (*lave emaillé*) to impart a shiny glaze that imitates the Asian porcelain so popular in the eighteenth century. Then each is painted using different oxides for coloration. A second firing fixes the design; an additional firing is needed to achieve certain bright colors. While some pieces are decorated freehand, more complicated designs are accomplished with a pattern, or *carton*—essentially tracing paper with tiny holes outlining the design. The artisan dusts black chalk over the holes with a brush, then removes the pattern to reveal a sketch, which is used as a guide for painting the final design.

After the French Revolution, with no more royalty or nobility to consume these luxurious wares, the industry declined, and the last fire in a Moustiers kiln was extinguished in 1878. However, a local impresario, Marcel Provence, restarted production in the 1920s, seeking to renew the tradition, and by the 1940s a renaissance of Moustiers ware was sparked. Today, a vibrant community of some two dozen accomplished *faïenciers* caters to visitors who come to this spot as much for its natural beauty as for its ceramics.

L'ORIGINAL

Some of the most authentic Moustiers wares are decorated with a clear blue known as *bleu de Clérissy*, named for the man who began the tradition of Moustiers ware.

ÇA COUTE COMBIEN?

If the prices seem steep in Moustiers, you'll understand why when you observe the long process and degree of precision involved in making these wares. Don't hesitate to ask an artisan to create a custom piece or service for you. Most are thrilled to create something personalized.

CRÈME DE LA CRÈME

Bondil (page 172) and Atelier Soleil (page 172) create the highest-quality wares in town.

FIGURINES

Santons

ook closely at the faces of the people of Provence, and you'll understand immediately where the tradition of *santons* derived. These doll-like fig-urines depict the characters and country folk of the region, from fruit sellers to laundresses, fair maidens, and town drunks. Once associated with the Christmas season but now popular year-round, *santons* are one of the most typ-ical Provençal crafts.

Santons, or "little saints" in Provençal, developed in Italy and came across the Alps to France sometime during the Middle Ages. Originally, they depicted saints and other religious figures, reproducing on a smaller scale the life-size crèches that were installed in churches throughout the region. People set up these little characters in their homes, where they illustrated Bible stories and acted as devotional aids.

Little by little, local color crept in. *Santonniers*, or *santon* makers, began to use local people as the model for these characters. Pretty soon, to the standard repertoire of saints and other religious notables were added fishmongers, lavender reapers, men playing *boules*, grandmothers carrying grandchildren, and a thousand other figures of people going about their daily tasks. By the seventeenth century, these characters attained their height of popularity, often set up in elaborate landscapes with miniature houses, dogs, horses, vegetable carts, and more.

As in the past, today *santonniers* carve these little marvels from wood, or more frequently, create them in terra-cotta using molds. Whether fully painted with oil-based or acrylic paints, or dressed in fabrics fashioned into traditional Provençal costumes, these petite figurines delight collectors. Many local Christmas festivals feature these fun characters, and are a great way to soak up Provençal culture. The Foire aux Santons in Marseille (page 182) is one of the best.

L'ORIGINAL
There is great variety in quality and price among Provençal *santons*, from slapped-together examples with little artistic merit, to more refined works. Most of those sold in tourist shops are not worth the money; stick to the few artisans singled out in this chapter to assure you're buying the best-quality and most authentic pieces.

COMBIEN CA COUTE?
Warning: collecting *santons* is habit forming. Passionate collectors can quickly sink a fortune into elaborate displays. Although you can spend just a few euros on a tiny terra-cotta figure, or many hundreds on a more elaborate model, if you enjoy these fun characters, chances are you can't buy just one.

CRÈME DE LA CRÈME
Ateliers Marcel Carbonel in Marseille (page 183) is one of the most famous *santonniers* in France, but it is hard to beat the truly exceptional quality of Daniel Scaturro, in the *santon* capital of Aubagne (page 181).

SOAP AND OLIVE PRODUCTS

Savon de Marseille

The bounty of olives in Provence has given locals reason to put every single part of these gnarled trees to good use. Woodworkers fashion many objects from the olive tree, from spoons to bowls and even furniture. Nutty-smelling olive oils, with their characteristic Mediterranean taste, flavor many of the regional dishes and form the basis for an infinite variety of beauty products and natural remedies, from lotions to hair dressings. And of course, the olives themselves are marinated with herbs and eagerly devoured by visitors and locals alike.

One of the most prized Provençal uses for olive oil is in soap making. *Savon de Marseille*, traditionally associated with this seaside city, is documented as far back as the twelfth century. The industry burgeoned in the eighteenth century, when it supported some five dozen soap makers in town. Strict laws dictated that only pure olive oil be used in its production. Soap making continued to flourish across southern France even after the French Revolution. In fact, it wasn't until the arrival of commercial detergents in the second half of the twentieth century that the soap-making industry went into decline, although a handful of artisanal soap makers still eke out a living in the region.

Savon de Marseille is based on a simple recipe, but its production is much more complicated than it might seem. The first step is to boil olive oil in giant cauldrons, which transforms it into a paste. The paste is then washed in water laced with sea salts. It sounds simple, but it's the cooking process that is artisanal and varies with each soap maker. Each artisan has his secrets: the mixture may go through several baths with different combinations of salted, cold, and warm water. The paste is filtered and left to rest for some thirty-six hours, and finally poured into molds. Next, it is cut into cubes and dried for several days. Each producer stamps his or her name on the soap blocks, which are usually square but sometimes rounded or rectangular.

Even in today's modern world, olive-oil soap is still valued for its moisturizing qualities, its purity, and its clean scent. Watching these old-fashioned soap makers at work is one of the pleasures of old Provence.

L'ORIGINAL

Most authentic savon de Marseille is composed of 72 percent olive oil, as is stamped directly on the block of soap.

ÇA COUTE COMBIEN?

Usually, savon de Marseille is priced by the gram; you'll pay between 5 and 10 euros for a typical block.

CRÈME DE LA CRÈME

La Compagnie de Provence in Marseille (page 180) brought savon de Marseille into the modern age, but a couple of old-fashioned soap makers in Salon-de-Provence (page 184) preserve the original techniques.

THE LISTINGS

PROVENCE–ALPES–CÔTE D'AZUR

Alpes-de-Haute-Provence

GRÉOUX-LES-BAINS

Gréoux-les-Bains is a refreshing old spa town in the hills north of Aix-en-Provence that makes for pleasant window-shopping.

CRYSTAL

J. Kubina
10 avenue des Marronniers
04 92 78 17 72

The inventory of this crystal shop is mostly tacky, but the crystal cutters put on an excellent show of their techniques on the sidewalk outside the store—a rare opportunity to watch crystal cutting in action.

POTTERY

Charrot
9 rue des Templiers
No phone

There's nothing traditional about the pottery in this workshop, but I find it just plain fun. Bright colors such as fuschia, turquoise, lime, and lemon all mix to create fun Provençal items at very reasonable prices. I chose a whimsical bowl for holding olives or nuts, as well as holders for tea-light candles.

SANTONS

Gérard Moine
36 avenue des Alpes
04 92 77 61 08
www.santonsmoine.free.fr

If you like kitsch, you'll love Gérard Moine's homemade sound-and-light extravaganza that tells the story of each *santon*—shepherds, men playing *boules*, women carrying bread, and more. Gérard's wife Martine sells the 5-euro tickets. For free, you can peruse the shop, which includes an exhibit of nativity figures from around the world.

MANOSQUE

HERBAL PRODUCTS

Magasin d'Usine L'Occitane
Zone Industrielle Saint-Maurice
04 92 70 19 00
www.loccitane.com

Mega-chain L'Occitane does not fit well in a book on artisans, but it is an icon of traditional Provençal products, and I'm sure you'll want to go to their factory store, so here's the scoop. The factory is conveniently located off the *autoroute*—easy to find and with plenty of parking. Discounts are relative to French retail prices, so chances are you will find similar prices in the United States on a good sale day, or at one of the U.S. outlet stores. However, I found a couple of good deals in the "seconds" section. The factory is not normally open to visitors, but if you have a group, you can call ahead to try to arrange a tour.

MOUSTIERS-SAINTE-MARIE

I'm a sucker for a good ceramics town, so Moustiers-Sainte-Marie is right up my alley. The combination of a stunning natural setting, a good choice of quality ceramics, and the chance to see artisans at work is a winning one. *Faïenciers* are located in small shops scattered around the village. The best strategy is to begin with the well-done Musée de la Faïence. Train your eye there, then weave through the village's narrow alleys to choose a souvenir that strikes your fancy. There are some two dozen *faïenciers* in Moustiers;

the ones listed below craft works of the highest quality, and follow the delicate feminine style of the seventeenth and eighteenth centuries most closely. Once you find a maker whose work you like, ask to see his or her atelier. Some are located in the historic center, others on the outskirts of town. Most ceramicists welcome visitors, and you can enjoy watching the complicated process of producing Moustiers ware firsthand. Moustiers-Sainte-Marie is far from anything, with twisty-turny narrow roads leading to it. My recommendation: splurge on the Bastide de Moustiers, Alain Ducasse's excellent inn and restaurant on the edge of town, so you can shop till you drop, take a dip in the pool, and then dine like a king.

FAIENCE

Art Provençal Le Cloître
Place Presbytère
04 92 74 62 03

Near the Office de Tourisme, this medieval setting is a great place for quality reproductions of historical Moustiers wares at fair prices of between 30 and 150 euros.

*Bondil
Place Pomey
04 92 74 67 02
Place Couvert
04 92 74 68 50

Hands down, Bondil produces the highest-quality wares in Moustiers, with intricate and refined painting, as well as some of the most faithful reproductions of historical pieces. Prices are steep, but if you want the best piece of faience in town, this is the place to buy it.

*Atelier Soleil
Chemin Marcel Provence
04 92 74 63 05
www.soleil-deux.fr

Soleil is another excellent *faïencerie,* located a little way out of town near the Bastide de Moustiers. Thank-you notes from five presidents of France and the United States grace the wall of this friendly atelier. With a diversity of styles, most of the work is fun, with bright

colors and motifs. One table contains seconds, some with nearly imperceptible defects, at good discounts. The service is extra-friendly, and the shop will ship to the United States.

Faïencerie Lallier
La Clape
04 92 74 60 73
La Forge
04 92 74 65 07
La Grotte
04 92 74 61 31

With three locations in town and a wide distribution elsewhere in France, Lallier is a decent-quality *faïencerie* where you can find affordable wares. I priced a lovely wall fountain for 400 euros, but smaller items like lamps, candlesticks, soap dishes, and plates will set you back much less than 100 euros and make a nice gift or souvenir.

Musée de la Faïence
Le Village
04 92 74 61 64

Even if you don't speak French, you can get a lot from the video that demonstrates the complex techniques involved in producing Moustiers ware. Then, go on to view the limited yet stunning collection of Moustiers ware from the sixteenth to the twentieth centuries—an excellent point of departure for a foray into the town of Moustiers.

RIEZ

Riez is a "real" French town, with limited tourism and a handful of good artisans who you can observe doing what they do best. On the way to the more heavily trafficked ceramics capital of Moustiers-Sainte-Marie (see page 171), Riez is worth a side trip.

FAIENCE

Faïencerie du Clocher
46 rue du Marché
04 92 77 87 28

Across from Riez's bell tower, this producer displays good-quality, refined Moustiers ware inside a homey stucco room with terra-cotta floor tiles.

SANTONS

Thierry Detrait
5 place Saint-Antoine
No phone

"*C'est une passion,*" Thierry Detrait tells me as he guides me around the nooks and crannies of his closet-size studio. For a quarter century, this *santonnier* has been crafting miniature houses, people, and accessories that no collector of Provençal *santons* should be without. The tiny cypress trees, so typically Provençal, are intricately crafted. Prices begin well below 100 euros but could add up if you start a collection.

Alpes-Maritimes

BIOT

Biot, an authentic old Provençal town with a respectable artisanal history, is unfortunately largely filled with tourist traps. Although most travelers come here to buy the bubbly glass that has made Biot a destination, the most traditional craft associated with the town is pottery.

GLASS

La Verrerie de Biot
5 chemin des Combes
04 93 65 03 00
www.verreriebiot.com

Though touristy, La Verrerie de Biot affords a great opportunity to see glassblowing in action. The large, airy showroom displays pieces like sets of barware and juice glasses to great advantage. Each piece is signed. Though I find this place to be a bit hokey, it's worth a stop for the chance to watch some thirty glass artisans at work and really understand the craft of glassblowing.

POTTERY

La Poterie Provençale
1689 route de la Mer
04 93 65 63 30

During the Middle Ages, the village of Biot, now known for glass, was famous for its huge urns, or *jarres*, some with handles, that were valued for transporting olives, nut oils, dried vegetables, wheat, and other foodstuffs. Most of the potters belonged to Ligurian families who populated Biot in the sixteenth century, each with a unique hallmark that was pressed into each jar. On the same street as the Fernand Léger museum, this is the oldest pottery establishment in town, and it strives to re-create the authentic *jarres* that once made Biot famous around the Mediterranean.

Musée d'Histoire et de Céramique Biotoises
9 rue Saint Sébastien
04 93 65 54 54

Here you can view original *jarres,* the famous wares of Biot that from the Middle Ages onward were celebrated for not altering the aroma or taste of their contents.

CANNES

Given that the city hosts an international cruise port and a convention center, not to mention the Cannes Film Festival, it's surprising that more artisans haven't set up shop here to cater to the many visitors. This city is all about glitz and glamour, and it is hard to find traditional regional crafts here among the big-name stores, including Chanel, Lacoste, and Louis Vuitton, that have opened along the waterfront and main shopping drags. However, the following are a couple of places where you can find authentic goods.

CANDIED FRUITS AND CHOCOLATE

Chez Bruno
14 rue Hoche
04 93 39 26 63
44 rue Georges Clémenceau
04 93 38 62 68

I nearly fainted when I couldn't find my favorite *chocolatier* on the rue d'Antibes, where it had sat since 1929. I had been dreaming of this shop's famous chocolate-covered orange peels for months! Fortunately, Bruno hasn't closed his doors, he just moved to a swankier locale on the rue Hoche. Try anything in the store and you'll be glad you made a stop. For

a gift, opt for a collection of chocolates in one of its signature wooden boxes. Its famous glazed chestnuts and clementine confits are so expensive (58 euros per kilo) and gorgeous that you may decide to decorate with them instead of eating them—if you can resist their charms!

FAIENCE

Lallier Moustiers
42/44 rue de Serbes
04 93 68 06 81

This is the Cannes outlet of a mid-grade ceramics atelier from Moustiers-Sainte-Marie (page 172). If you can't make it to Moustiers, this is not a bad place to pick up a souvenir.

GRASSE

Grasse's historic center is a picturesque jumble of medieval alleyways, while the modern town sprawls in all directions with views over a countryside of red-tiled roofs, palm trees, and verdant hills, and glimpses of the glistening sea beyond. Don't let the tour buses put you off. Grasse is actually less touristy than some other Provençal destinations. There is enough of "real France" here to make your explorations interesting.

JEWELRY

*Musée Provençal du Costume et du Bijou
2 rue Jean Ossola
04 93 36 44 65

Provençal fabrics come to life in this wonderful small museum run by the Fragonard perfume empire, and a stop here is a must for the creative display. Dramatically lit mannequins clad in traditional Provençal costumes of the eighteenth and nineteenth centuries are encased and suspended in glass cylinders, evoking the dolls you see at the duty-free shops and tourist strips of Paris. The jewelry is large, colorful, and fun—ornate jeweled crosses are threaded on ribbons around the mannequins' necks. To buy reproductions of what you see here, head to Fragonard Maison (see below).

Fragonard Maison
2 rue Amiral de Grasse
04 93 40 12 04

I love this store, which focuses on scents and home decor items related to the Fragonard perfumery. Especially appealing are the historical reproductions of the nineteenth-century jewelry displayed in Fragonard's costume museum down the street. Enormous jeweled crosses and other pendants on black satin ribbons, as well as cabochons, sell for less than 100 euros. Beautiful heirloom-quality baby gifts in fine linen also make this shop a winner.

PERFUME

*Parfumerie Fragonard
20 boulevard Fragonard
04 93 36 44 65
www.fragonard.com

Fragonard enjoys the most prominent presence of the three big perfume makers here, and does a lot of business with tour companies that park their buses at the lower entrance to the perfumery. Founded in 1912, the Costa family still runs this operation (the name Fragonard was taken in honor of the eighteenth-century painter who was born in Grasse). The museum is fascinating and clearly shows the steps of the perfume-making process, which is done by

hand (or at least partly so). The copper alembics used to distill the essential oils are artisanal masterpieces in themselves. Other interesting displays include antique soap presses, centuries-old treatises on scents, and beautiful incense burners and perfume flasks made of silver, crystal, enamel, even a mussel shell. In the shop, the legions of salespeople can help you choose among several lines of floral fragrances, as well as soaps, home scents, and more. Look for the *échantillons*, tiny white strips on the countertops on which you can spray test samples. Belle de Nuit is its famous brand, a floral scent available in bottles for 33 to 50 euros.

Musée International de la Parfumerie
8 place du Cours
04 93 36 80 20
www.museedegrasse.com

Call ahead to check the status of this excellent perfume museum, which has been closed for an extensive renovation.

Galimard
73 route de Cannes
04 93 09 20 00
www.galimard.com

Jean de Galimard, who once supplied the royal court as a glove and perfume maker, founded this enterprise in 1747. With a shop in a modern factory outside of town, Galimard's unique offering, aside from perfume, is a full line of yummy-smelling soaps. You can sample its goods as well in its small showroom near the overlook in the center of Grasse.

Molinard
60 boulevard Victor Hugo
04 93 36 01 62
www.molinard.com

Molinard, in a large château a short walk down a busy street from the center, has a fascinating exhibition of historical perfume containers, or *flacons*, made by Baccarat and Lalique. This cavernous, bright shop displays its line of scents in pretty purple packaging on antique Provençal tables. Compared to Fragonard's floral notes, the fragrances of Molinard are sharper and more acidic; Habanita is its signature perfume. You can attend a create-your-own-scent workshop for 40 euros.

NICE

The Monday flea market on the cours Saleya in the Old Town quarter is a great place to scout for antique artisanal objects—vintage jewelry, enamel boxes, pottery, and heavy silver serving pieces that previously graced Provençal hotels and restaurants. For a town of its size, Nice boasts several very good old-fashioned stores that will transport you to old Provence.

CANDIED FRUITS

Confiserie Auer
7 rue Saint-François-de-Paule
04 93 85 77 98
www.maison-auer.com

Founded in 1820, the Confiserie Auer retail space preserves the original decor, from the fancy woodwork to the sales counters. Thankfully, it also preserves the original recipes for typical candied fruits and luscious chocolates, made in the *laboratoire* behind this ornate shop. The *confiserie* remains in the Auer family after five generations, and has become a Nice institution.

Confiserie Florian de Vieux-Nice
14 quai Papacino
04 93 55 43 50
www.confiserieflorian.com

If you're not able to make it to Florian's evocative factory near Tourrettes-sur-Loup (following page), pick up its signature candied or sugared fruits, wrapped in gorgeous packaging, for a special gift.

OLIVE PRODUCTS

Nicola Alziari
318 boulevard de la Madeleine
04 93 44 45 12

Although there are countless olive mills across Provence, Nicola Alziari's is special for its history and location in the historic center of Nice. Not so long ago, locals brought their own containers to fill with oil from the giant vats in this mill. Today, you can observe the oil extraction process, and enjoy a tasting, or dégustation, on-site. There is a smaller shop at 14 rue Saint-François-de-Paule, which sells a selection of oils as well as bowls and implements hand-carved from olive wood.

LINENS

Les Olivades
8 avenue de Verdun
04 93 88 75 50
www.les-olivades.com

Surprisingly affordable in this neighborhood of Hermès, Lacoste, and Vuitton, this nice Les Olivades store displays napkin holders tied at the edges, skirts and other clothes, and pillows for well below 50 euros. You can also buy cloth by the meter. The store carries a few other home decor items that are typical of Provençal style, from egg cups to select ceramic tableware and lamps.

POTTERY

Terre è Provence
7 rue Masséna
04 93 16 93 45

See listing, page 184.

SAINT-PAUL-DE-VENCE

Saint-Paul-de-Vence is almost perfect, which explains why it's been almost ruined by tourism. Saint-Paul is a high-class tourist trap, its medieval alleys crammed with exclusive art galleries and, of course, crafts. This too-adorable cobblestoned village contains a couple of luxury inns and hosts a litany of summer events that attract the European and American jet-set. By all means, enjoy Saint-Paul-de-Vence. Just be aware that very little is actually crafted here. Everything is made somewhere else and brought to the shops to be sold at top prices to international visitors. Below are a few places where you can find quality handmade souvenirs.

FURNITURE

Senator
80 rue Grande
04 93 58 73 49

Furniture fit for a château is the specialty of Senator. The company's atelier is based in Nice, where its *ébénistes* craft gorgeous reproductions of period-style chests, chairs, and other accent pieces, many with marquetry. Silk and velvet cushions and drapes round out its royal inventory. The company ships much overseas, so it can negotiate special rates for you. Considering what you pay for the actual piece (I drooled over a Louis XVI-style commode for 5,000 euros), the shipping will be a drop in the bucket.

PROVENÇAL FABRICS

Kallisté
55 rue Grande
04 93 32 70 60

This little interior design shop includes some nice *boutis*, the quilted bedspreads of Provence, including some by the renowned regional fabric company, Souleiado. A king-size *boutis* will set you back about 225 euros. The helpful staff can also help you pick out quality pottery.

Provence Boutis
37 bis Grande Rue
No phone

This below-street-level shop, no more than a cellar, displays some stunning, high-quality *boutis* from across southern France, reasonably priced between 30 and 90 euros.

TOURRETTES-SUR-LOUP

Tourrettes-sur-Loup is a lovely medieval town that has been cleaned up for the many tourists who wander its narrow alleys exploring the ateliers of the three dozen painters, weavers, sculptors, and potters who have set up shop here. There's nothing very traditional, but a few of the stores sell quality artisanal wares. The best strategy is to wander the Grand'Rue, which snakes around the periphery of town and affords stunning views over the Provençal countryside.

CANDIED FRUITS

Confiserie Florian
Pont de Loup (outside Tourrettes-sur-Loup)
04 93 59 32 91
www.confiserieflorian.com

Although it's touristy, this is a fun place to sample the famous Provençal candied fruits and see how they're made. The factory, founded in 1921, sits in a gorge outside Tourrettes-sur-Loup, alongside the river Loup. You can watch the *confiseurs* turning oranges, lemons, tangerines, plums, and even violets into delectable treats. A free guided tour and tasting let you sample the crispy-sweet crystallized fruits. For a memorable experience, sit at one of the tables in the verdant garden, and try the violet or lavender ice cream.

OLIVE WOOD CRAFTS

DuBosq et Fils
4 Grand'Rue
04 93 24 11 70

My hunt for a beautiful salad bowl and utensils crafted of olive wood ended here in the little studio of DuBosq. It also displays hundreds of other miniature items in olive wood, including cutting boards, trays, and small sculptures. A nice bowl with utensils runs around 200 euros. On commission, larger items, including furniture, can be created.

POTTERY

Arnaud Chassaing
1 Grand'Rue
04 93 59 27 92

Potter Arnaud Chassaing crafts nice quality, traditional Provençal wares—most are utilitarian plates, bowls, pitchers, flasks, and other vessels for the table. The deep, rustic blues and earth tones help set a table with a distinctively Provençal accent.

WEAVING

Atelier Arachnée
8 Grand'Rue
04 93 24 11 42

You'll be drawn in by the pure charm of Michèle Badets, as well as by the quality and beauty of her weavings. Self-taught, Badets is an able weaver and charismatic host; her studio sits back from the cobblestoned Grand'Rue as it descends into a maze of crooked alleys. You'll find her working at her loom (a reproduction of an antique model), or showing clients her colorful collections of ladies' suits, hats, scarves, sweaters, and shawls, in wool, silk, and cotton. Prices are steep: I fell for a fuschia skirt and jacket combination that would have set me back more than 500 euros.

VALBONNE

Valbonne is a quiet, picture-perfect *bastide* town, laid out by medieval city planners as a fortified grid of alleys. Today the setting makes a perfect home for traditional craftspeople of all stripes.

PERFUME BOTTLES

Création Boselli
13 rue Grande
04 93 60 11 81

Perfume bottles made of exotic woods comprise the niche craft of Jean-Pierre Boselli. This Provençal artisan began as a sculptor of the native olive wood, but soon began experimenting with more exotic imported woods from as far away as Cameroon, Brazil, and Morocco. Hidden inside each beautiful wooden receptacle is a glass flask that holds the perfume.

PORCELAIN

Pupilles et Papilles
18 bis rue de la Mairie
04 93 12 29 14
www.chauffaille.com

Parisian Denis Chauffaille left the big city behind for life as a small-town artisan a decade ago, and has established a wonderful niche for himself in this craft town. His specialty is pure white porcelain with refined, delicate designs, which he creates on-site in his Valbonne workshop. His passion is for custom tableware and decorative items.

POTTERY

Atelier Barocco
29 place Arcades
04 93 12 92 35

In the small workspace at the back of this shop, you can watch Monsieur Barocco craft good-quality, hardy utilitarian tableware. Serving plates, bowls, pots, pitchers, and flasks with blue, brown, and green tones pair perfectly with utensils crafted of rich olive wood.

VALLAURIS

Vallauris is known for two kinds of pottery: ancient and modern. Rustic, utilitarian wares have been made here for some two thousand years. In the 1940s, Pablo Picasso began collaborating with a local ceramicist and made Vallauris the center of a modern ceramics community; you can see some of his original works at the Galerie Madoura. The town also hosts a small ceramics museum and a bienniale that awards prizes to ceramicists. Despite this impressive heritage, sadly, Vallauris is mostly a disappointment, as tacky tourist traps selling inferior wares dominate the main drag, the avenue Georges Clémenceau, and only a couple of shops are worth a stop.

POTTERY

Foucard-Jourdan
65 avenue Georges Clémenceau
04 93 63 74 92

Foucard-Jourdan stands out in Vallauris for
the quality of its rustic tableware. Its forte is
glazed, almost iridescent casseroles in browns,
golds, and greens. Its wares spill out from the
shop into the courtyard, next door to the
Galerie Sassi-Milici (see below).

Galerie Sassi-Milici
65 bis avenue Georges Clémenceau
04 93 64 65 71
www.sassi-milici.com

If you want to go home with a reproduction
of one of Pablo Picasso's ceramic creations—
and money is no object—shop here. Vallauris's
most famous gallery sells reproduction Picasso
plates for around 8,000 euros, as well as
large-scale contemporary ceramic works.
The large, elegant gallery is housed in an
old ceramics factory built in 1852. It ships
to the United States.

Lou Pignatier
43 and 52 avenue Georges Clémenceau
04 93 64 65 38

Bright and fun, the ceramics of Lou Pignatier
include oven dishes with domed lids, cups,
saucers, and plates in bright colors at reasonable prices. This is one of the town's more
acclaimed potters, and he has received several
prizes at the bienniale.

Bouches-du-Rhône

AIX-EN-PROVENCE

Aix-en-Provence makes me nostalgic for my
university days in France. The town is full of
college students, fountains, lovely tree-lined
streets, and thankfully, some good craft shopping, too.

BAKED GOODS

Béchard
12 cours Mirabeau
04 42 26 06 78

One of the oldest bakeries in town hawks its
specialty wafflelike cookies, or *gaufrettes*. There
are many other gorgeous and tasty goodies to
drool over as well, including beautiful ice-
cream tarts with glazed fruits, chocolates,
pastries, and more artful treats.

Confiserie Entrecasteaux
2 rue Entrecasteaux
04 42 27 15 02

This is an excellent place to buy *calissons d'Aix*,
the town's typical candied almonds, made in
Aix-en-Provence since the fifteenth century.
Have them all wrapped up in a beautiful
almond-shaped red box.

LINENS

Souleiado
8 place des Chapeliers
04 42 21 06 32
www.souleiado.com

This branch of Souleiado specializes in table
linens, with a more limited selection of home
linens. I purchased a quilted throw pillow
cover on sale for 12 euros.

Sud Etoffe
57 rue Espariat
04 42 26 55 58
www.sudetoffe.fr

This regional company runs several inviting shops across the south. Here you will find excellent *boutis*, placemats, napkins, table linens and small delectables. Some of the goods are made by hand, while others are machine finished—ask the staff to show you which is which. I purchased some colorful mix-and-match napkins that I use for entertaining.

L'Esprit des Lieux en Provence
10 rue de Gaston de Saporta
04 42 21 20 74

Down the street from Souleiado, this company claims to sell *ambiance de la maison*, and it is, indeed, a seductive design showcase. Intermixed with more mass-produced items are a few artisanal wares: handmade ceramics, typical Provençal *boutis*, table linens by Le Jacquard Français, a few *santons*, and some of the most gorgeous chandeliers I've ever seen. Prices are high: you'll pay 12 euros for a single napkin. It ships around the globe.

POTTERY

Terre è Provence
6 bis rue Aude
04 42 93 04 54

See listing, page 184.

SANTONS

Michel Girault
35 rue Bédarrides
04 42 27 17 35

Handsome Michel Girault works at a small table surrounded by shelves stacked to the high ceilings with neatly organized molds (*moules*) for *santons*. An adjacent room displays the small finished figures painted with bright colors, starting at 9 euros. The larger ones, dressed in Provençal costume and engaged in activities like playing *boules* or carrying produce, go for 44 euros. The studio is located one floor above street level.

Santons Fouque
65 cours Gambetta
04 42 26 33 38
www.santons-fouque.com; www.santons-fouque.fr

Located on the edge of town, this rather touristy destination is worth a detour if you're a fan of *santons*. The atelier's claim to fame is a figure with the title *"coup de Mistral,"* which depicts a man straining against the strong wind, the infamous mistral that blows through Provence every year. Paul Fouque crafted this mold in 1952, and his daugther, Mireille Fouque, has carried this character into today's production, as well as a host of others from her grandfather and father's generations.

SAVON DE MARSEILLE

La Compagnie de Provence
63 rue des Cordeliers
04 42 27 37 41

This is the Aix location of the well-regarded Marseillais company that took humble *savon de Marseille* to a new level with its sleek boutiques (page 183). This one carries the traditional long blocks and perfect squares of olive-oil soap, as well as liquid soap in clear dispensers, and hand and body lotions made with lavender and olive oil.

TABLEWARE

Jacquèmes
9 rue Méjanes
04 42 23 48 64
www.jacquemes.fr

If you are a gourmand or like to entertain guests, you will love this place. In addition to mouthwatering gourmet treats and an outstanding selection of wine and liqueurs, Jacquèmes has assembled a top-notch array of artisanal tableware from all over France. There is a quality selection of handmade Laguiole and Nontron knives, corkscrews, crystal decanters from Lorraine, and other goodies.

ARLES

Arles retains the air of a bullfighting town, dominated by the ruins of its great Roman amphitheater. You won't be surprised to learn that designer Christian Lacroix hails from Arles, because it's here that the southern ladies' costumes reached their fanciest and most baroque elaboration: full skirts of black, yellow, and red taffeta, with ruffles, lace, and ribbons showing underneath. *Bijoux arlesiennes*, extravagant hammered gold and gem jewelry, finished off the look, which you can catch a glimpse of during the annual Fête d'Arles in May.

JEWELRY

Li Beloio
11 rue Porte-de-Laure
04 90 49 64 33

This quaint shop within view of Les Arènes, the Roman-era amphitheater that looms over Arles, deals in unique antique pieces of typical old jewelry from Arles, *bijoux arlesiennes*. On commission, you can also have a reproduction made—a fabulous souvenir from Arles.

Bijouterie Pinus
6 rue Jean Jaures
04 90 96 04 63
www.bijoux-pinus.com

Pinus re-creates pieces of *bijoux arlesiennes*, including stunning hammered gold necklaces and bracelets, some with red garnets and other gems. This family business has also revived many other Provençal jewelry designs, which, centuries ago, used to be as individual as each town.

LINENS

Souleiado
4 boulevard des Lices
04 90 96 37 55
www.solieado.com

The Souleiado branch is located across the street from the Arles Office de Tourisme. In this branch, the emphasis is on brightly colored shirts, skirts, jackets, and other accessories in true *arlésienne* fashion, though the store carries the usual table linens as well.

AUBAGNE

As a town, Aubagne is a bit rough around the edges, but a visit to Daniel Scaturro's atelier makes it all worthwhile. Some thirty *santonniers* are scattered around Aubagne, which has grown into the center of *santon* production. You will pay less here for one than elsewhere.

SANTONS

*Daniel Scaturro
20A avenue de Verdun
04 42 84 33 29
www.santonsdanielscaturro.com

If you're serious about buying a high-quality *santon*, look no further. Daniel Scaturro is the undisputed master of the Aubagne *santon*. If you've browsed elsewhere, once you see Scaturro's work, you'll understand the difference: the faces are finely modeled, the expressions more realistic, the painting more refined. You can buy an off-the-shelf model starting at around 40 euros. Scaturro has created portrait *santons* for French presidents, including François Mitterrand. For 1,000 euros, you can commission him to create a *santon* of you or someone you love, based on photographs. In the boutique, exhibitions display crèches old and new. Scaturro founded and is the president of an international society of *santonniers* that seeks to unite these artisans from around Europe.

Le Petit Monde de Marcel Pagnol
Esplanade Charles de Gaulle
04 42 03 49 98

Playwright and filmmaker Marcel Pagnol, whose stories centered around the characters and landscapes of southern France, is Aubagne's most famous native son. This exhibition, a tribute to the author, is a mind-blowing display of some two hundred figures, all crafted by *santonniers* in Aubagne, representing the characters of Pagnol's works.

MARSEILLE

Marseille is a big city, and there's not much cute or quaint about it, in spite of its seaside location. Still, it is home to several of the country's most beloved makers of *santons* and soap, and is worth a stop. With traffic, crowds, and urban sprawl, decide which shops you want to visit, then hail a taxi to take you directly to your destination.

GENERAL CRAFTS

Maison de l'Artisanat et des Métiers d'Art de Marseille
21 cours Honoré d'Estienne d'Orves
04 91 54 80 54
www.maisondelartisanat.org

This administrative seat of the regional artisan chamber of commerce boasts a beautiful street-level space devoted to rotating exhibitions featuring crafts from France and abroad. It has mounted shows of Provençal fabrics, *savon de Marseille*, perfume bottles, handmade boats, wine decanters, and more, so it's worth a visit to see what's on display.

NAVETTES MARSEILLAISES

Le Four des Navettes
136 rue Sainte
04 91 33 32 12
www.fourdesnavettes.com

One of the region's most traditional sweet treats, *navettes marseillaises* are cookies with a hint of orange, shaped in the form of a shallow boat. They evoke the legend of Mary Magdalene, Marie-Salomé, and Martha—who reportedly landed their craft at Sainte-Marie-de-la-Mer, near Marseille, to Christianize Provence in ancient times; the event is commemorated on February 2 each year. Several bakeries in town specialize in these tasty cookies, but Le Four des Navettes is the oldest bakery in Marseille, founded in 1791.

PORCELAIN AND FAIENCE

Figuères et Fils Société
10–12 avenue Lauzier
04 91 73 06 79
www.faiencerie-figueres.com

Platters piled high with stunningly realistic ceramic fruit are the specialty of this little studio. Its artisans also make platters with shellfish and vegetables—again, all of faience—that are really cool. The shop is located on a side street in Marseille's more pleasant beachside district, east of the city center. It's a stone's throw from the faience museum, and the two make a nice excursion for ceramics fans.

Musée de la Faïence
Château Pastré
157 avenue Montredon
04 91 72 43 47

The faience museum contains more than a thousand pieces of faience from ancient times to the present, including impressive pieces of Marseille faience from the eighteenth century, all lovingly displayed in a château near the beach.

SANTONS

Arterra
1 rue du Petit Puits
04 91 91 03 31
www.santons-arterra.com

On a street of potters in the maze of Marseille's Old Town quarter, Arterra stands out for offering a twist on standard Provençal themes. For one, its *santons*—even the big ones—are fully painted, not clothed in fabric like most. You can watch *santonniers* at work at their tables in the showroom. Having seen many gaudy ceramic *cigales*, the cicadas that are a symbol of Provence—I was excited to buy more tasteful wooden ones. Prices are reasonable here: 3 to 25 euros for *cigales*, 5 to 500 for *santons* in bright colors. There is also a small selection of *boutis* and placemats for 8 to 15 euros.

Ateliers Marcel Carbonel
47–49 rue Neuve Sainte-Catherine
04 91 54 26 58
www.santonsmarcelcarbonel.com

Carbonel is one of the most well-known *santonniers* in the country. In the boutique, across from the workshop, there is a nice exhibit of *santons* from Italy, Spain, and elsewhere, and an informative display showing the molds (*moules*) and final figures. Call ahead to arrange a visit to the atelier. In the shop, *santon* prices start at 9 euros and go up.

SAVON DE MARSEILLE

La Compagnie de Provence
1 rue Caisserie
04 91 56 20 94
18 rue Francis Davso
04 91 33 04 17
www.lcdpmarseille.com

Two smart former Marseillais sunglass designers turned a nonglamorous craft into a sleek, well-marketed object of desire with their hip boutiques in Marseille and elsewhere (page 180). A local factory makes soap for the company, employing techniques very close to the ancient methods.

SAINT-RÉMY-DE-PROVENCE

I love Saint-Rémy-de-Provence, and I think you will, too. It's authentic, easy to navigate, and has a lot of charm. The rue Lafayette cuts a course through the round medieval village, and it's there you'll find some of the region's best-loved names in *santons*, *boutis*, and pottery.

GENERAL CRAFTS

*Le Grand Magasin
24 rue de la Commune
04 90 92 18 79
www.le-grandmagasin.com

Warning: impulse buys ahead! A treasure-hunter's dream, this is an absolutely fun store. Whimsy sums up this emporium of jewelry, sculpture, paintings, and other objects that defy categorization. Everything in this shop is handmade and one-of-a-kind. My own impulse buy was a bracelet made with the keys of an antique typewriter.

CANDIED FRUITS AND CHOCOLATE

*Joel Durand
3 boulevard Victor Hugo
04 90 92 38 25
www.chocolat-durand.com

If you're a chocoholic, you'll think you've died and gone to heaven when you enter this shop. As soon as you open the door, the aroma is overwhelming, wafting from a chocolate fountain. Joel Durand has created an alphabet of chocolate pastilles—each letter with a different flavor, from orange to rosemary, lavender, honey, mint, and more. I chose the letter O since I like orange (you eat the letter, too as it's made of cocoa)—as well as chocolate-coated roasted almond clusters that were the best I've ever tasted. Shipping is available.

Lilamand
5 avenue Albert Schweitzer
04 90 92 11 08
www.lilamand.com

This venerable *confisier* has been supplying locals with candied fruit since 1860. The old factory stands beside the showroom, with crystal chandeliers and an elegant serpentine counter. Pumpkin-shaped jars contain mixed fruit in syrup.

LINENS

Les Olivades
28 rue Lafayette
04 90 92 00 80
www.lesolivades.fr

This branch of Les Olivades, on the main square, displays items better than its other stores, and it is a good place to purchase a gift—like a signature scarf for just under 100 euros, or a shirt or bed linens.

Souleiado
2 rue Lafayette
04 90 92 45 90
www.souleiado.com

The Saint-Rémy location of Souleiado presents a particularly alluring display, including brooches and doorknobs featuring the ubiquitous *cigale* of Provence, as well as several dozen bolts of its signature fabrics, chic tote bags, shirts, and table linens, *bien sûr*.

POTTERY

Terre è Provence
1 rue Lafayette
04 90 92 28 52

Terre è Provence is a regional chain offering quality handmade tableware. Its factory, located in the nearby Drôme region, employs a legion of potters but relies on an entirely handmade process. One specialty is the *cigales* (cicadas) that can be used as spoon rests, and the larger sized ones that you can hang on the wall, which are more elegant than the ones you see littering the tourist shops around Provence. I like the square serving dishes in the typical tones of gold, blue, and umber. Choose a tray embellished with olives, a set of cereal bowls, or a small plate for pouring olive oil and dipping bread. You can spend as little as 7 euros for a miniature *santon*, or as much as a couple hundred euros for a soup tureen. The company also has shops in Aix-en-Provence (page 180), Avignon (page 187), and Nice (page 176).

SALON-DE-PROVENCE

If you like sophisticated merchandising and efficient shopping, buy your soap at l'Occitane and La Compagnie de Provence. But if you want to step back into the nineteenth century and experience how savon de Marseille is produced firsthand, head to the quiet town of Salon-de-Provence, where two producers of savon de Marseille continue a tradition of soapmaking. First, stop at the Office de Tourisme—well-marked as you enter town—to get a map showing the locations of these two establishments. Both are situated west of the historical center in a nondescript part of town.

GENERAL CRAFTS

Musée Grévin de la Provence
Place des Centuries
04 90 56 36 30

The museum traces the history of Provence and some of its popular traditions. The gift shop carries a few *santons* crafted by Santons Fouque (see page 180), Aix-en-Provence's mostly highly regarded *santonnier*.

SAVON DE MARSEILLE

Rampal-Patou
71 rue Félix Pyat
04 90 56 07 28
www.rampalpatou.com

Yes, it's okay to enter. The "shop" of this establishment consists of some shelves in the back of the factory floor in this no-frills establishment that has changed little since 1828. A *savonnier* feeds blocks of soap into an electric press that cuts them into round shapes and dispenses them out the other side, where he then loads them into a tray. You can buy raw blocks of soap, or small gift boxes or mesh bags tied with ribbon and lavender for around 10 euros. I put together a lovely gift of a dozen small squares of soap in different scents, including lavender, olive oil, and even *pamplemousse* (grapefruit).

Savonnerie Marius Fabre
148 avenue Paul Bourret
04 90 53 24 77
www.marius-fabre.fr

A little more upscale than Rampal-Patou (though that's not saying much), Fabre, founded in 1900, is another place where you can observe the process of soap making, now in its third generation of family operation. There is also a small museum devoted to savon de Marseille, where you can see fascinating old metal stamps for soap, as well as a store. Call ahead to make sure it's open and reserve a tour, usually offered twice a week. This is one of those places that sometimes closes during the posted opening hours.

TARASCON

LINENS

Magasin d'Usine Les Olivades
Chemin des Indienneurs
Saint-Etienne-du-Grès (outside Tarascon)
04 90 49 19 19
www.lesolivades.com

On the outskirts of Tarascon, the factory store of Les Olivades lies close to its country roots, a wooded spot alongside pastures with an occasional wandering donkey or goose. The unassuming two-room factory store displays a haphazard but well-priced selection—shirts for 50 euros, ties for 29. I even scored a tablecloth for 10 euros.

*Musée et Magasin d'Usine Souleiado
39 rue Proudhon
04 90 91 50 11
www.souleiado.com

There's an incongruous combination of austerity and gaiety that is the key to Provençal style. Until I visited the Souleiado museum in Tarascon, I didn't fully understand it. This museum encapsulates it perfectly, and if you want to delve into the tradition of *indiennes*—the brightly printed fabrics synonymous with Provençal style—this is the place to do it. Here you can see a fascinating display of the wood-blocks—incredible examples of *artisanat provençal* in themselves—used to create the fabric prints, and a re-creation of a paint-mixing laboratory, as well as examples of regional dress through the centuries.

The factory store offers prices approximately 30 percent below the other Souleiado shops. More contemporary, stylish tops are mixed in with traditional *indiennes*. The children's clothing is a highlight. Clearance items are in the back of the store. Some local friends warned me that the service is notoriously curt, but personally I did not find this to be the case.

Var

COGOLIN

RUGS

Manufacture des Tapis de Cogolin
Boulevard Louis Blanc
04 94 55 70 65
www.manufacture-cogolin.com

Elton John, Bill Gates, Charles de Gaulle, and the sultan of Oman figure among the clientele of this custom-only maker of carpets outside Saint-Tropez. Since 1924, Manufacture des Tapis de Cogolin has used antique looms from Aubusson (chapter 4) to hand-craft one-of-a-kind floor coverings for spaces as diverse as the Elysees Palace to yachts and private jets. It also has a showroom in Paris (chapter 1).

SAINT-TROPEZ

LEATHER SANDALS

K. Jacques
25 rue du General Allard
04 94 54 83 63
16 rue Seillon
04 94 97 41 50
www.lestropeziennes.com

Leather craftsman Kéklikian Jacques opened a boutique on the rue Allard in 1933, selling handcrafted sandals and developing a reputation for custom-made sandals for the jet-set film industry clientele who frequented Saint-Tropez and docked fancy yachts in the harbor. Known as *spartiates tropeziennes*, today the shoes are synonymous with this seaside resort. Still in the Jacques family, a more spacious shop on the rue Seillon offers a wider gamut of stylish shoes. The craftsmen have created shoes for Karl Lagerfeld, Kenzo, and other couture houses. A pair of sandals runs 100 euros and up.

Rondini
16 rue Georges-Clémenceau
04 94 97 19 55
www.rondini.fr

In his little atelier behind this shop, Alain Rondini continues the artisanal tradition of his father Serge and grandfather Dominique, who opened this shop in 1927 to offer hand-crafted sandals to visitors and residents of Saint-Tropez. Rondini remains a high-quality producer of calf-colored leather sandals. It ships to the United States for about 20 euros a pair.

SALERNES

One of the oldest continuously operating pottery towns in Europe, artisans in Salernes have been working the soil for a mind-boggling seven thousand years! These days, the town is an important center of ceramic tiles. Some are large-scale industrial producers of floor tiles for domestic use and export, while others retain a more artisanal base.

CERAMIC TILES

Alain Vagh Ceramique
Route d'Entrecasteaux
04 94 70 61 85
www.alainvagh.fr

A bizarre spiral ceramic obelisk marks the workshop of Alain Vagh, one of the town's most creative tile makers. Across the street from the factory, the showroom contains bright tile displays for kitchen and bath, many with hand-painted scenes and custom work. Vagh does wonders with color.

Poterie Salernoise
Route de Draguignan
04 94 70 64 82
www.poteriesalernoise.com

The multilingual staff at Poterie Salernoise can tell you more about the high-quality, lustrous traditional and contemporary ceramics in their shop, many of which have undergone a laborious enameling process to give them a gorgeous sheen. The shop is on the round-about leading to Draguignan.

AVIGNON

Avignon is a wonderful town for strolling and soaking up regional history. Unfortunately, individual artisans are largely absent, but the big names in Provençal style and tradition are well represented.

GENERAL CRAFTS

*Mistral, Les Indiennes de Nîmes
19 rue Joseph-Vernet
04 90 86 32 05

If you want people to wonder if you are a matador, or perhaps an international movie star, this is a great place to find the right outfit. This company uses eighteenth- and nineteenth-century fabrics and *objets* from the area as inspiration for a full line of fancy skirts, tops, vests, hats, and home decor with a truly authentic and alluring Provençal flair. The main level showcases clothes; upstairs, there are one-of-a-kind decorations and tableware. It's hard to sum up this visual feast of Old Provence in words—you have to see it to believe it.

LINENS

Souleiado
5 rue Joseph Vernet
04 90 86 47 67
www.souleiado.com

In addition to the regular Souleiado fare, this branch carries lovely reproductions of old-fashioned Provençal jewelry, including large crosses on black ribbons for around 40 euros.

Sud Etoffe
Place du Change and 156 route de Tarascon
04 90 82 72 95

See listing, page 179.

POTTERY

Terre è Provence
26 rue de la République

See listing, page 184.

Vaucluse

L'ISLE SUR LA SORGUE

L'Isle sur la Sorgue, a village east of Avignon, is a major regional antiques center. Put this town on your itinerary for a weekend, when there is a fabulous market and all the shops have their doors open. Of course, you can't go with your mind set on any one particular item, since this kind of shopping is treasure hunting at its best. On any given day, you might unearth a century-old ceramic pitcher, a wrought-iron garden gate, a lustrous inlay table, or a piece of vintage sterling silver. Below are a couple of the town's most interesting finds, but the best strategy is to browse and enjoy.

BOUTIS

Michel Biehn
7 avenue des Quatre-Otages
04 90 20 89 04
www.michelbiehn.com

Michel Biehn is well-known in France for his expertise in regional textiles, as well as his ever-changing display of Provençal objects of the past. Biehn began collecting antique Provençal *boutis* after spending a decade in Asia looking at fabrics. He boasts an important collection.

WROUGHT-IRON WORKS

Bossard
37 cours Emile Zola
04 90 20 70 17

Erick Bossard deals in masterpieces of antique wrought iron, a métier practiced less and less these days. Look for kitchen accessories, fireplace grilles and grates with decorative curls and swirls, and smaller, more portable items.

A Year of French Tradition:
Calendar of Events

The sheer number and variety of festivals across France each year is staggering. Whether it's the arrival of *nouveau Beaujolais* wine, the display of elaborate creches at Christmas, or the emergence of tender asparagus stalks in June, it seems that almost every local tradition is reason to celebrate. Traditional crafts often take center stage at these annual events, so it's a great opportunity to soak up the best of French artisanship. In addition to the events listed below, be sure to check with the local tourist offices. Look for events called *artisans sans vitrines* or *ateliers ouverts*, one-time opportunities to visit artisan studios that are normally closed.

JANUARY

17
FAYL-BILLOT, CHAMPAGNE
FÊTE DE SAINT-ANTOINE

Festival of Saint Anthony, patron of basket makers.

FEBRUARY

FIRST WEEK
TOULOUSE, MIDI-PYRÉNÉES
FESTIVAL DES VIOLETTES

Festival of Violets, including crafts made with them.

2
MARSEILLE, PROVENCE
FÊTE DE LA CHANDELEUR

Feast of the Three Maries, featuring *navettes marseillaises* cookies.

APRIL

MID-MONTH
BAYONNE, AQUITAINE
FOIRE AU JAMBON DE BAYONNE

Fair of Bayonne Ham, awarding prizes for the best cured ham, since 1426.

MAY

BEGINNING OF THE MONTH
ARLES, PROVENCE
FÊTE D'ARLES

Festival of Arles, featuring traditional local costumes.

THIRD WEEK
VILLAINES-LES-ROCHERS, CENTRE
SALON DES ARTIVANNERIES

Basket-Making Festival, featuring local weavers.

JULY

FIRST SUNDAY
ARLES, PROVENCE
FÊTE DU COSTUME

Costume Festival, displaying historical dress *à l'arlésienne*.

SECOND WEEK
COGNAC, CHARENTE-MARITIME
FÊTE DE COGNAC

Festival of Cognac, showcasing the town's major producers.

MID-MONTH
PONT L'ABBÉ, BRITTANY
FÊTE DES BRODEUSES

Embroidery Festival, featuring outlandish costumes and *coiffes*.

AUGUST

FIRST WEEKEND

DIGNE-LES-BAINS, PROVENCE
CORSO DE LA LAVANDE

Lavender Festival, celebrating the fragrant flower and everything imaginable made with it.

FIRST WEEKEND

GRASSE, PROVENCE
FÊTE DU JASMIN

Jasmine Festival, featuring the prized flower for perfume making.

FIRST WEEK

NONTRON, PÉRIGORD
LA FÊTE DU COUTEAU

Knife Festival, featuring Nontron's historic knives.

THIRD WEEK (BIENNIALLY)

SAINT QUENTIN LA POTERIE, GARD
FESTIVAL EUROPÉEN DES ARTS CÉRAMIQUES

Ceramics Festival, featuring ceramic tableware and decorative objects from throughout Europe.

SEPTEMBER

FIRST SUNDAY

SOUFFLENHEIM, ALSACE
GRANDE FÊTE DE LA POTERIE

Great Pottery Festival, showcasing rustic Alsatian wares.

LATE

SALON-DE-PROVENCE, PROVENCE
JOURNÉE DE L'OLIVIER EN PROVENCE

Olive Days, featuring olive-related food and crafts.

LAST WEEKEND

MARTRES-TOLOSANE, MIDI-PYRÉNÉES
FÊTE DE LA FAÏENCE

Faience Festival, featuring the fancy local wares.

NOVEMBER

LAST WEEK
TARASCON, PROVENCE
MARCHÉ AUX SANTONS
Santon Market, showcasing the work of regional *santonniers*.

LAST WEEK *(and first week of December)*
AIX-EN-PROVENCE, PROVENCE
FOIRE AUX SANTONS
Santon fair, featuring Provençal figurines.

LAST WEEK
CHAMBÉRY, SAVOIE
FESTIVAL DES MÉTIERS DE LA MON-
TAGNE
Mountain Craft Festival, celebrating local food, bells, furniture, and woodcrafts.

DECEMBER

BEGINNING OF MONTH
GIEN, CENTRE
VENTE ANNUAL
Annual auction of Gien faience.

FIRST TWO WEEKS
ARLES, PROVENCE
SALON INTERNATIONAL
DES SANTONNIERS
Santon Festival, assembling *santonniers* from Provence and beyond.

ALL MONTH
KAYSERSBERG, ALSACE
MARCHÉ DE NOËL
Christmas Craft Festival, featuring ornaments, nativities, and holiday food.

ALL MONTH
MARSEILLE, PROVENCE
FOIRE AUX SANTONS
Nativity fair (the region's largest), featuring a vast array of Provençal *santons*.

ABOUT THE AUTHOR

Laura Morelli is an art historian and writer with a passion for the world's artisanal traditions. Morelli has lived and worked in several countries in Latin America and Europe, including four years in France. She holds a degree in Romance Languages, and earned a Ph.D. in Art History from Yale University. She has taught at Trinity College, Tufts University, and Northeastern University, and has lectured to public audiences across the United States and Europe. She is the author of *Made in Italy* and *Made in the Southwest*, both published by Universe.

For more information, visit www.lauramorelli.com.